JESUS FOR A NEW MILLENNIUM

A Savior
sufficient for
Earth's last days

KEN WADE

Pacific Press® Publishing Association
Nampa, Idaho
Oshawa, Ontario, Canada

Edited by Jerry D. Thomas
Designed by Dennis Ferree
Cover art by Nathan Greene

Copyright © 1999 by
Pacific Press® Publishing Association
Printed in the United States of America
All Rights Reserved

Unless otherwise noted, all Bible texts are quoted from the
New King James Version.

ISBN 0-8163-1761-5

99 00 01 02 03 • 5 4 3 2 1

CONTENTS

FOREWORD

Expectations. We all have them. My wife Jeannie and I recently sat on the runway in a DC-10, awaiting takeoff. Next stop, home! We couldn't wait. We waited expectantly—for nearly four hours. What to do? The plane was packed. Overbooked, in fact. Mothers with small children ran out of "surprises" and things to keep small hands occupied. Flight attendants began to disappear into the mysterious little elevator in the kitchen, fleeing to the nether regions of the cargo area, safely out of reach of frustrated passengers. People demanded answers. Some sulked because they couldn't order liquor. We couldn't even snack on peanuts because by law everything had to be kept under lock and key until after takeoff.

At last the captain's voice crackled over the intercom, "Sorry folks. Mechanical problems." Then the dreaded news. Flight canceled . . . no more flights today.

Jeannie and I finally limped home nearly two days later after a comical cavalcade of errors, broken promises, and alternate itineraries.

What about delay? Christ's promised space trip, that is. If, after nearly 2,000 years of flight delays, you've begun to wonder whether Jesus will ever come again, you are in for some pleasant surprises and flight reports in this book.

I've noticed that few books have forewords these days. But I'm so glad my friend and colleague, Ken Wade, invited me to share a few quick tips about the journey you're about to embark on before you take the plunge and turn the page.

Ken is good at what he does. He's one of the finest Christian wordsmiths around, and you're about to discover why we're so pleased that he recently joined our Voice of Prophecy broadcast team as a writer/producer. You will like this book.

We all remember the O. J. Simpson trial in Los Angeles. It droned on far too long, but millions of Americans stayed glued to their television sets. We were John Q. Public, sucked into the vortex of a real-life courtroom drama, sitting on front-row seats with Judge Lance Ito and attorneys Johnny Cochran, Marcia Clark, and Chris Darden. Everyone who witnessed even a portion of their theatrics remembers the intrigue and subterfuge. We not only became members of the jury but were challenged to become detectives in this case. Experts. Consumed with the all-important phrase: "Consider the evidence!"

Ken Wade asks us to do the same thing with questions that affect all of us. Even if you feel that you already understand the Bible's prophecies about your future, this book challenges you to probe deeper into the subject of end times. Deeper than most people bother to go. Ken takes a closer look at some very important questions. And comes up with solid answers.

So fasten your seat belts. You're about to be reintroduced to a Savior who loves to do more for us than we could ever expect. One who loves to exceed our expectations. The evidence is there. Jesus *will come through!*

E. Lonnie Melashenko
Speaker-director, Voice of Prophecy

CHAPTER 1

Dupes?

Are Christians the biggest bunch of dupes the world has ever seen? I mean, they've been waiting almost 2,000 years for a promise to be fulfilled, and they just keep hanging on, like they expect it to be fulfilled tomorrow.

Let's put it this way: If you had a good friend who walked out of your life one day, promising to return and take you to where he was going, what would you expect? How long would you wait? And then, suppose that while your friend was away, he wrote you a letter and the last thing he said in the letter was, "One thing I want you to know for sure—I'm coming quickly!" What would you expect? Would you start watching the street in front of your house? How long would you keep watching? For a week? A month? A year? A decade?

How soon would you get discouraged and give up? How soon would you begin to assume that either something had gone drastically wrong or that your friend wasn't very trustworthy? If you could live for a century, would you wait that long and still keep believing in your friend's trustworthiness? How about a millennium? Or how about two millennia?

And let's say you had managed to hang onto your faith and to wait a decade or two. Would you still be able to face the neighbors who had seen you sitting out on your front porch, peering eagerly down the street as your hair gradually changed from jet black to silver? How would you respond to their jabs and lighthearted comments? How would you feel when you saw them out in their driveways glancing your way then guffawing and slapping each other on the back?

Wouldn't you begin to feel like a dupe, a patsy, an outcast? Would you eventually, in order to regain your sense of sanity, join in with the neighbors in making jokes about your friend's promises?

Then why is it that there are hundreds of millions of Christians in the world who still cling to the hope that Jesus of Nazareth is going to come back again? He left nearly 2,000 years ago.

He hasn't come back yet. Even though He sent a message to His best friend, John, more than 1,900 years ago saying "Surely I am coming quickly," He still hasn't made good on the promise. Have these hundreds of millions of people abandoned their senses? Is there some unknown disease that has eaten away portions of their brains, robbing them of the ability to see the truth of their situation?

Look at the evidence

Before we make any rash accusations, let's take a look at the evidence. Did Jesus of Nazareth (better known as Jesus Christ, which means Joshua the Anointed One) promise to come back, and if so, in what terms? Is it possible that people have merely misunderstood what He said and that the Christians' hope is built up out of incorrect assumptions and false expectations?

What did Jesus actually promise to do?

One of His most familiar promises is found in John 14:1-3, which records words He said near the end of His time on earth. As He introduced His disciples to the concept of His upcoming departure, He said, " 'Let not your heart be troubled; you believe in God, believe also in Me. In My Father's house are many mansions; if it were not so, I would have told you. I go to prepare a place for you. And if I go and prepare a place for you, I will come again and receive you to Myself; that where I am, there you may be also.' "

That's pretty clear and straightforward, isn't it? And I mean, how long could it take for Him to prepare that place? If He's the Son of God, shouldn't He have been able to complete the task by now?

Jesus spoke those words at a time when His disciples were expressing concern because He had begun to talk about leaving them. They clearly refer to His upcoming departure and to what would happen afterward. But this promise doesn't say anything about how quickly Jesus planned to return. If this was all He had ever said about returning, such an open-ended promise could refer to any time in the future—even several more millennia from now.

But that wasn't all Jesus had to say about His return. He also said this: " 'For the Son of Man will come in the glory of His Father with His angels, and then He will reward each according to His works. Assuredly, I say to you, there are some standing here who shall not taste death till they see the Son of Man coming in His kingdom' "(Matthew 16:27, 28).

Probably based on that statement, many early Christians held out strong hope that Jesus would return within a few decades of His departure. In fact, by the time all the disciples except John had died, the rumor arose that Jesus had promised that He would return while John was still alive. Near the end of his life, John wrote the account of the life of Jesus that we call the Gospel of John. In closing that Gospel, John put that rumor to rest with these words: "Because of this, the rumor spread among the brothers that this disciple would not die. But Jesus did not say that he would not die; he only said, 'If I want him to remain alive until I return, what is that to you?' " (John 21:23, NIV).*

About this time also, John had a vision of Jesus, which is recorded in the last book of the Bible, the book of Revelation. In closing that vision, Jesus made this statement about His plans to return: "He who testifies to these things says, 'Surely I am coming quickly' " (Revelation 22:20).

Having looked at the evidence from Jesus' own testimony, you might be ready to close the case. To declare all Christians patsies and dupes who still expect Jesus to fulfill His promise to return soon. Fools who can't face the reality of unfulfilled expectations and get on with their lives.

But if you're ready to close the case that quickly, it must be because you've never read a good detective story. As any fan of good mysteries knows, the opening scene of the story is only intended to set the stage—to present certain elements of evidence that all point to what seems a foregone conclusion. The job of the detective on the case is to look over the scene carefully and then to go looking for the details and clues the average eye misses.

I'd like to challenge you to be the detective on this case.

There is more evidence to consider. Evidence that may vindicate the Man who promised to come back. But it's not to be found on the surface. You have to dig deeper. Deeper than most people ever bother to go.

Got your gumshoes on? Magnifying glass in hand? Sherlock cap and cape? Then let's start digging. The first thing we're going to go looking for is character evidence.

---

*See appendix for my understanding of what Jesus meant when He said that some would not taste death before they saw the Son of Man coming in His kingdom.

Should we even take this case? Is there any good reason to believe that we can believe our client, Jesus of Nazareth? Any reason to trust His claim to be the Savior of the world, who will return with the gift of eternal life for those who believe in Him? Any reason to carry hope for His *soon* return with us into the third millennium since His birth?

CHAPTER 2

The Surprising Savior

Based on the kind of evidence we looked at in chapter 1, many people have gotten discouraged waiting for Jesus to come. Years ago, when I was in college, my wife told me about a visit she'd had with an elderly gentleman who had lost his hope. "When I was a young boy," he told her, "I expected Jesus to come any day. I've been hoping He'd come for the past eighty years. But now I don't believe it anymore. I just can't believe it. It's been too long."

Some people might respond to his loss of faith by saying something like, "Well, welcome to the real world at last! Finally you've woken up and come to your senses!" But is that how we should react? And if not, why not? After all, we Christians have been preaching the soon return of Jesus for nearly two thousand years.

But we're still here.

Jesus hasn't lived up to our expectations.

And it's easy to get discouraged when people don't meet our expectations.

Is there any good reason why we shouldn't give up our hope?

I've had to face that question seriously a number of times. I pride myself in being a careful researcher, willing to face the evidence and follow it wherever it leads. But sometimes I've found myself just skipping past certain texts, afraid of the conclusions they might take me to.

Finally, though, I couldn't go on that way any longer. I had to take a closer look at Jesus and the things He said.

It's that kind of closer look I'm inviting you to take with me.

One of the things I discovered about Jesus that I find helpful in trying to understand what He said and His plans for the future is that He loves to pull surprises on people.

In fact, I've come to believe that Jesus is almost a bit of a practical joker!

Don't believe it?

Before you pass judgment and toss this book away, please consider a few pieces of evidence. I think they'll not only help you understand Jesus better. They'll help you understand what He promised to do and what you can expect from Him in the third millennium.

Let me hasten to add that I don't mean that Jesus is the kind of joker who would put a bucket of water above your door so it would fall on you as you came into your house. He's not the kind of person who would short-sheet your bed or put Limburger cheese on the manifold of your car. But He does have a penchant for pulling off surprises.

As we build our character evidence file, let's look at a couple of stories about Jesus. Remember, we're playing detective here. Let's try to reconstruct the evidence as best we can and discover what it reveals about the character of the Man in question, Jesus of Nazareth.

We'll begin with the story told in the eleventh chapter of the Gospel of John.

Character evidence: story one

Some of Jesus' favorite friends on earth were Mary, Martha, and Lazarus—two sisters and their brother, who lived in the little town of Bethany, just a stone's throw from Jerusalem. They were the kind of people Jesus enjoyed "hanging out" with. It seems as though He could go to their house and feel comfortable just kicking back and enjoying good conversation.

The story in John 11 starts out as a tragedy. Sickness, fever, gasping for breath, delirium, and finally the peaceful but terrifying rest of unconsciousness. It's Lazarus who is suffering all these things. The sisters and other friends gather around his bed, praying, weeping, wondering what more they can do. And of course someone asks, "Where's Jesus these days?"

It's a natural question in such circumstances, because Jesus has earned a reputation as the best healer since Elisha. There are documented cases of His having gone into villages and healed every illness there, starting with the common cold and working up through the flu, pneumonia, ulcers, blindness, and epilepsy, all the way to the most fearsome cases of demon possession.

It wasn't hard to find out where a celebrity like Jesus was spending His time. People coming up the road from Jericho talked about Him constantly. Mary and Martha soon learned that He had gone down through Jericho and crossed the Hajlah Ford across the Jordan River and set up camp in the same area where John the Baptist had held his evangelistic campaign a few years back.

The place was only about a day's journey away.

Once they found out where Jesus was, it wasn't long until a neighbor volunteered to make the trip to summon Jesus. "Hurry!" Martha urged as the man mounted his donkey. "Tell Jesus that the physicians have given up hope. Ask Him to come as soon as He can. Lazarus can't last much longer!"

The man sped off on his plodding donkey, headed down

the road into the gorge that was known as the Valley of the Shadow of Death. It was the road that figured prominently in the story Jesus had told of the good Samaritan. It wasn't a bad place to travel in daylight, but woe be to the pilgrim who didn't make it out of the dark canyons and into the Jordan plain near Jericho by nightfall!

While the man traveled, in search of Jesus, Lazarus entered his own valley of shadows.

The neighbor made it to Jericho and on across the Jordan by late afternoon. It wasn't hard to find Jesus. You just had to follow the crowds. He hastened toward the Master healer with his report.

Jesus listened carefully to the description of Lazarus's vital signs then rendered His diagnosis: " 'This sickness will not end in death' " (John 11:4, NIV). The glad tidings lightened the neighbor's countenance immediately, and the rest of what Jesus said may not have even registered with him. It didn't seem relevant anyhow. It was just something about how Lazarus's illness was for the glory of God.

The man was no doubt tempted to turn his donkey around then and there and hurry back to Bethany with the good news, but if he was wise, he thought better of it and stayed the night with Jesus and the disciples or perhaps found lodging back in Jericho, at the foot of the mountains. From there he would be able to get an early morning start on the treacherous uphill trip to Bethany.

Jesus, meanwhile, went on about His business, teaching and preaching and healing complete strangers. His disciples, knowing everything was under control in Bethany, probably gave little further thought to Lazarus's illness.

As the neighbor hastened into Bethany with his good news late in the afternoon of the following day, he was puzzled to hear the sounds of wailing growing louder and louder as he approached his neighborhood. Worse yet, when he arrived at Lazarus's house, he discovered that the noise was coming from inside. What could it mean? Had some other tragedy befallen the family in his absence? He knew the wailers couldn't be mourning for Lazarus—Jesus had said *his* illness wouldn't end in death.

But they *were* mourning for Lazarus. Lazarus was dead!

And the good news—the words he had brought from Jesus—seemed a mockery now.

"This sickness will not end in death." He muttered the words under his breath as he made his way inside. The funeral bier was almost ready for its terminal trip by the time he found Mary. Distraught, she looked at him. "Did Jesus come with you?" she pleaded.

"No . . . Uh, He said He didn't need to come just yet. He said . . ."

"He said what?" it was Martha who had come up behind, who posed the question. "What did Jesus say?"

"He said . . . um . . ." the man, overcome with his own grief at the loss of a dear friend and overwhelmed by the powerful emotions surging around him among the mourners, couldn't think of what to say. His hand flew up to cover his mouth, to stifle the wail that pulsed in his lungs, and he ran, stumbling, almost falling, out the door, fleeing into the fresh air.

But Mary, the one who had often sat at Jesus' feet, hanging on to His every word, could not let the man go without telling her what Jesus had said. She pursued him all the way out to the front gate and laid her hand on his shoulder to stop his flight.

Finally regaining his composure, he turned to face her. Her tear-streaked face looked hard, almost angry, but her chin quivered as she spoke. "What did Jesus say?" she demanded.

The man turned to face her, his eyes full of hurt, compassion, and confusion. At first he couldn't speak, but Mary's eyes pled with him for some word from the Master. Finally, his head hanging, his eyes looking down to where the woman's hands fidgeted with her robe, he spoke. "He told me to come on back. That the sickness wouldn't end in death."

He raised his head then and looked her full in the face again. Her eyes were full of pain, and it seemed like words were about to explode from her quivering lips, but she turned and ran back into the house, her wails setting off a new round of mourning from the gathered troupe.

Aghast, Mary faced the greatest contradiction and greatest disappointment of her life. She had to face the reality that even Jesus could be wrong sometimes. Or worse yet, was it possible that He had lied—glossing over the seriousness of the situation to save His own skin, because He was afraid to come back up to the neighborhood of Jerusalem because He knew the authorities there were out to kill Him?

She sank down into bitter confusion and despair at the realization that Jesus was not all He claimed to be. That the one Man other than her brother that she had thought she could trust had just proven her wrong.

Remember. This was the woman Jesus had redeemed from a wayward life of prostitution—the one whose life He had spared when the Pharisees wanted to stone her—the one from whom He had cast out seven demons.

She had learned through the years to trust Jesus.

But now He had let her down.

Meanwhile, down by the Jordan, Jesus did nothing. Made no move or comment to indicate that anything was amiss up in Bethany. In retrospect, friends would say that He had remained curiously aloof from the neediness of some of His most devoted friends. As if suffering and life and death among those He cared most about didn't really matter at all. Finally, two days later, without saying any more about Lazarus, He suggested to His disciples that they ought to cross the Jordan and head back up toward Bethany and Jerusalem.

His suggestion didn't meet with any enthusiasm, for more reasons than one. Foremost in the disciples' minds was the fact that the last time they'd been in Jerusalem Jesus had gotten into serious trouble with the law—had had to leave like a fugitive to avoid being stoned to death. Then again, spring had just begun to dawn upon the mountains, warming them up from their winter chill. They'd spent the past several months down in the sunny, subtropical Jordan Valley. Couldn't a trip up the mountain wait at least till the weather warmed up a bit?

Only after the disciples objected to the trip did Jesus bother to explain. " 'Our friend Lazarus sleeps, but I go that I may wake him up,' " He said (John 11:11).

Still the disciples objected. "After all," they argued, "if he's sleeping, that's good. It'll help him recover faster."

Finally Jesus had to explain that Lazarus was dead. Then He said a curious thing: " 'For your sake I am glad I was not there, so that you may believe' " (John 11:15).

It seemed an odd thing to say, and no one was quite sure why He said it. Nothing about it motivated them to want to hurry up the hill. Prospects of the trip through the Valley of the Shadow of Death to the dangerous environs of Jerusalem just hadn't been part of their plans for the immediate future.

It was Thomas (who would later be known as The Doubter) who expressed the sentiment that carried the day. "Come on, let's go with Jesus," he said. "We might as well die with Him."

Finally, on the second day after Lazarus had died—long after His friends had expected Him to come—Jesus set out to do what needed to be done to glorify God.

By the time He finally got to Bethany, Lazarus had been dead for four days. By the way people counted days back then, that could mean that Lazarus had died on Monday and Jesus arrived on Thursday.

Martha was the first to hear of His arrival on the outskirts of town. I can picture her—active woman that she was—leaping to her feet, pushing her way through the crowd of sympathizers who were still making a show of mourning, and hurrying down the road toward Jericho. Ready to give Jesus a piece of her mind!

There He was, coming up the road at a leisurely pace, seemingly unconcerned. She broke into a run and came bustling to a stop directly in front of Him. " 'Lord,' " she said, a mixture of frustration and grief making her voice quaver, " 'if You had been here, my brother would not have died' " (John 11:21).

Jesus seemed at first not to respond but only looked at her with that calm, resolute gaze that spoke of peace with His Father and peace with the events that the Father chose to bring into His life. The gaze took its effect on Martha, and she looked down, then up again, sensing in the eyes of Jesus a power that could handle even this tragedy. Then she hastened to add, " 'But I know that even now God will give you whatever you ask' " (John 11:22).

Mary soon appeared on the scene, and the two sisters told Jesus about the burial and who had come to mourn. They said they wished that He could have been there for His friend, before it was too late.

And then at last Jesus entered fully into the emotion of His friends. "Jesus wept," says the shortest verse in the Bible.

Even though He knew what He was going to do next, Jesus felt compassion for those who were suffering. His aloofness down in the valley did not spring from apathy but simply from having a different response than what people expected. A better response. But now He shed real tears, entering into their grief and sense of loss.

But even as the tears glistened in His eyes, there must have been a twinkle there as well. For He knew the joke He was going to play on the old enemy Death. And He knew the joy and laughter that would fill that place when He was through.

In the sisters' eyes, Jesus had delayed His coming.

In their eyes, He had proved unfaithful to His word.

And it did seem that He arrived a few days late.

Yes, it seemed to be four days late when Jesus arrived in Bethany. Four days late when He spoke to Lazarus. But in the long run, it really didn't matter much.

Jesus had not met people's expectations. He had exceeded them. For when He finally did speak, Lazarus rose from the dead and walked out of his tomb. Jesus proved that He had been truthful all along. The illness did not end in death. Death claimed only a brief interlude in the life of Lazarus.

But how the faith of Mary and Martha and all of Lazarus's friends must have been tested as they passed through that dark hour—the valley of the shadow of death and the time of uncertainty as they waited for Jesus to come.

How they must have questioned *why* Jesus didn't come when they expected Him to.

Do you see why this story is important evidence for us to consider as we, who wonder why Jesus hasn't come yet, build a character profile of Him?

If you're having doubts about Jesus, if you're wondering whether He really will come again as promised, reread John 11.

There's something special here.

It's a clue about the character and the plans of Jesus. It can give us something to hang onto when things seem dark and our expectations are unrequited.

Notice this about Jesus:

He was seldom swayed by the expectations of mortals—not even by the seeming needs and suffering of His closest friends. He had a plan. Always had a plan. Always a better plan than what people expected. And He always fulfilled that plan, *exceeding* people's expectations. He delighted in exceeding people's expectations.

There's another story about Lazarus's sister Mary that illuminates the same aspect of Jesus' character. Another surprise. Another practical joke, if you can accept it.

Character evidence: story two

It happened after Jesus had been crucified. Once again, He had failed to live up to people's expectations. He had let them down majorly! People had staked their lives, their hopes of the future, on Him as the leader who would free their land from oppressors. Many had left their homes, given up their businesses to follow Him, depending on Him to lead them and provide for them.

And then, on a Friday afternoon, He had suddenly checked out on them. Gotten Himself killed! And now they were in turmoil far worse than what had engulfed Martha and Mary when they sat staring at Lazarus's corpse, repeating over and over the promise of Jesus that this illness wouldn't end in death.

Confused and distraught, Mary stumbled her way on Sunday morning down to the garden where Jesus had been buried. She needed time to think, time to sort out all that had happened to her and to the Man who had given her back her dignity.

On Friday evening the Romans had hastily granted permission, just before the coming of the Sabbath at sundown, to bury Jesus in a rich man's tomb. By rights, because He had died a criminal's death, His body ought to have been cast to the mangy dogs that prowled the depths of the garbage pits in the Gehenna Valley. But some influential Jews had made arrangements for this special body to be given a decent burial in a nearby garden.

When Mary arrived at the garden on Sunday morning, she discovered to her horror that the stone protecting the front of the tomb had been rolled away. Looking inside, she discovered that Jesus' body had been removed!

She could only imagine the worst: that the Romans had decided that no one who died on a cross was worthy of a decent burial. That they had come during the night and dragged the body, ignominiously through the streets, and flung it off a cliff into the dump where the dogs would have their way with it.

She ran and found two of the disciples, who ran back to the tomb with her. It wasn't yet light enough to see much, but they went into the tomb and found the empty burial shroud. After that they seemed in a hurry to get away from the place, and they rushed off.

But Mary tarried, unwilling to leave.

She stood outside the tomb, weeping as morning broke around her. Finally, as the shafts of daylight pierced the gloom, she took one last look inside.

And now Jesus set His joke—His surprise—in motion. I can almost see Him standing off in the shadows, watching, weeping with Mary once again as He sees how deeply the despair of losing Him has moved her. But watch those eyes! Once again there's a twinkle among the tears!

Then, just as Mary bends to take one last, longing look at where her Savior and Friend had lain, Jesus issues an order to the angels who had been there all along, and they make themselves visible to human eyes. Through her tears, Mary sees two men dressed in white inside the tomb. "Why are you weeping?" they ask.

When she tells them about the disappearance of Jesus' body, they seem unconcerned, so she simply turns to leave.

Is Jesus grinning now in the shadows, as He thinks about what He's going to do next?

On her way out of the tomb, Mary finally sees Jesus. But her red and sodden eyes don't recognize Him. She thinks He's just a gardener. He asks her why she's crying and who she's looking for, and she replies as one would speak to a servant, with her back turned, asking Him to simply tell her where the body had been taken.

Jesus can't wait any longer. Finally He springs His surprise. "Mary," He says in the way He had done so many times before.

And suddenly the joke is complete. Mary's sobs once again are turned to laughing.

Jesus is alive! Resurrected just as her brother had been!

Oh, day of weeping, oh day of laughter, oh day of exultation, oh day of . . . every emotion known to man!

The Savior is alive.

He has not disappointed us.

He *will not* disappoint us.

Once again Jesus has exceeded Mary's expectations!

In wild ecstasy she runs from that place to proclaim that yet again a stone had been rolled away and a Man had walked away from death.

The evidence: our story

Has Jesus failed to live up to our expectations?

Should He have returned a long, long time ago?

Have we had our hopes dashed time and again?

Are we standing, weeping at the empty tomb, wondering how we could have been so wrong about Jesus—to trust Him?

The stories we've looked at, from John 11 and John 20, give character evidence about Jesus. Looking at the evidence, we get a glimmer of new hope. Maybe—no, *probably*—He has another surprise in store for His friends.

We're not the first people to misunderstand the prophecies about His intentions—as we'll notice in the next chapter.

CHAPTER 3

Not What They Expected

" 'Behold, I will send you Elijah the prophet before the coming of the great and dreadful day of the Lord' " (Malachi 4:5). For a Jew living in Palestine in A.D. 27, these words carried the same weight as the next-to-the-last verse of the New Testament to a Christian in A.D. 2000: "He who testifies to these things says, 'Surely I am coming quickly.' Amen. Even so, come, Lord Jesus!" (Revelation 22:20).

The Jews in A.D. 27 looked hopefully forward to the fulfillment of Malachi's prophecies. They longed for the return of Elijah, but even more, they longed for the coming "day of the Lord" when everything would be set right in Israel, when God would come suddenly and purify His people and restore their former glory. Malachi's prophecies looked forward to that time too:

"Behold, I send My messenger, and he will prepare the way before Me. And the Lord, whom you seek, will suddenly come to His temple, even the Messenger of the covenant, in whom you delight. Behold, He is coming," says the Lord of hosts. But who can endure the day of His coming? And who can stand when He appears? For He is like a refiner's fire and like fullers' soap. He will sit as a refiner and a purifier of silver; he will purify the sons of Levi, and purge them as gold and silver, that they may offer to the Lord an offering in righteousness. Then the offering of Judah and Jerusalem will be pleasant to the Lord, as in the days of old, as in former years (Malachi 3:1-4).

The long, hot summer of the fourteenth year of Emperor Tiberius was drawing to a close in Jerusalem. Things had pretty well settled down to normal again after the arrival of the new Roman procurator, Pontius Pilate, the year before. Pilate had made the obligatory tour of the country, stopping by Jerusalem, but then had retreated back to the more comfortable and progressive environs of Caesarea by the sea—the beautiful seaport that Herod the Great had built forty years previously.

As the civil calendar ticked off Tiberius's fourteenth year, another calendar that had been counting days and years for nearly half a millennium was moving inexorably toward its climax. This was the prophetic calendar of Daniel 9, which pointed to the time when the Messiah would come.

The time was at hand.

But Pilate knew nothing of this.

For the most part, the procurator left the running of Jerusalem and the rest of Judea to the council of priests, Pharisees, and other leaders known as the Sanhedrin. And under their leadership things ran smoothly. Caiaphas, the high priest and head of the council, had been in office for nearly ten years and usually kept things under tight control. Sure, there had been a few uprisings in recent years. Every once in a while some bandit or other scoundrel would stir up some trouble, preaching that the time had come to overthrow the Romans. But the Sanhedrin could usually handle those kinds of problems without much help. The priests, after all, knew that their positions and authority were a gift from the Romans. They had a lot of investment in the status quo and weren't about to let anything dislodge them from their positions of power.

For the past twenty years, ever since Emperor Augustus had deposed Herod the Great's son Archelaus and appointed Coponius as the first procurator of Judea, the high priest hadn't even been able to perform any of his most important ceremonial duties without approval from Rome. The priestly vestments—the robes that he wore on annual high days like the Day of Atonement—were kept locked up in the Roman Antonia fortress, which overlooked the temple grounds. So the priests knew that if they didn't keep the crowds who came for the high days under control, the Romans could quickly shut down the ceremonies.

In other words, the very continuance of their religion relied on permission from Rome.

Nonetheless, the crowds on special days could easily get unruly. If things got too hot for the Sanhedrin to handle, they could always appeal to the Roman commander who maintained his headquarters in the Roman fortress. Since Judea was a Roman province, governed by a procurator, there was not a full legion on hand. A smaller auxiliary co-hort was usually all that was needed. The nearest Roman legion was stationed up in Damascus, several days' march away.

Pilate knew how to deal with anyone who might threaten the peace and security of his realm, and for their part the Sanhedrin seemed glad to have him, and willing to help maintain the Pax Romana—the peace of Rome. They didn't expect to see the procurator back in Jerusalem until sometime in September, when the annual blowing of the trumpets, Day of Atonement, and Feast of Tabernacles would bring throngs of faithful Jews to town. Pilate would come then, with an extra platoon of troops, just to make sure things stayed calm.

The olive harvest was almost over. Oil—the symbol of the Spirit of God—was flowing freely from presses on the Mount of Olives. Fresh dates and summer figs were beginning to show up in the market. With any luck, the early rains of autumn would soon settle the dust that filled the air. All seemed to be going well.

Then the priests got the word.

Trouble at the Jordan

Down by the Jordan. Over on the other side, in the area known as Perea, people said a prophet had appeared. The laypeople were getting excited. They were hurrying down the road to Jericho and on across the Jordan River, "Like flies descending on rotten meat," one scornful scribe said. From the reports coming back up the hill to Jerusalem, it sounded as though the situation could quickly become critical if it wasn't handled properly. This "prophet" was quoting texts like Malachi 3:1: " 'Behold, I send My messenger, and he will prepare the way before Me' " and Isaiah 40:3: "The voice of him that crieth in the wilderness, 'Prepare the way of the LORD, make straight in the desert a highway for our God.' "

People who hoped for deliverance from foreign powers had been using those texts for centuries to stir up trouble.

Now it was happening again.

Having a purported prophet stir up the crowds to believe that the Messiah had come, or was soon to come, was about the worst nightmare the priests could imagine. Such excitement always boded ill for peace and prosperity. If Roman troops had to be called to action, it would bring no end of trouble and suffering.

Perea was outside Pilate's jurisdiction. It was controlled by one of the sons of Herod the Great named Herod Antipas. But anything that happened among the Jews, whether in

Judea, Galilee, Perea, or even in Rome, had to be overseen by the Sanhedrin. So it wasn't long before the priests had appointed some representatives to go over to Perea to check things out and, hopefully, to verify that this man wasn't claiming to be the long-awaited Messiah.

They found the prophet just across the river. The people called him John the Baptizer because he preached about repentance and took people down and dunked them under the water to purify them from their sins.

The priests and Levites got right to the point as soon as they found John. " 'Who are you,' " they asked (John 1:19).

John must have been expecting them. He knew what they wanted. They weren't asking for his name. They wanted to know if he was claiming to be the Messiah, so he answered their implied question: " 'I am not the Christ' " (John 1:20).

That didn't satisfy them. They had heard him quote from Malachi 3, and they well knew that those texts were tied to the texts at the end of the book about Elijah the prophet coming just before the day of judgment. They wanted to know more.

They pursued him further: " 'What then, are you Elijah?' " they asked. When he assured them that he was not, they still continued their questioning. " 'Are you the Prophet?' "— referring to the special prophet that Moses had promised would come someday, who would also be regarded as a sign that the day of the Lord's judgment had arrived (see Deuteronomy 18:15-18). But John assured them he was not laying claim to that title either.

That seemed to mollify the priests a bit, but they still needed to fill out a report to take back to Jerusalem, so they asked him just exactly what he had to say about himself.

They weren't ready for his answer.

It scared them.

They knew it wouldn't reassure anyone back at head-quarters.

He couldn't have upset them more if he had announced a Roman legion was about to sack Jerusalem and defile the temple.

To the priests and others who held the reigns of power in Jerusalem, the text John quoted was terrifying. It meant disorder, disruption, and danger.

" 'I am the voice of one crying in the wilderness, "Make straight the way of the Lord," ' " John said (John 1:23; see Isaiah 40:3). The significance of that text was not lost on his interrogators. They knew that just two verses farther down the same prophecy proclaimed that "the glory of the LORD shall be revealed, and all flesh shall see it together: for the mouth of the LORD hath spoken it" (Isaiah 40:5).

I would have liked to have been there to hear the report the priests brought back to the Sanhedrin. "Well, at least he's not claiming to be the Elijah or the Messiah," they must have consoled themselves.

"But what about that quotation from Isaiah?" someone asked. "To me that's tantamount to claiming to be the one preparing the way for the Lord to come—to being the one preparing Israel for the day of judgment. Don't you realize how dangerous that is—especially with the Day of Atonement just around the corner and Pilate making plans to be here in town! In the people's minds, the Day of Atonement equals the Day of Judgment! We'd better put a stop to it before the Roman commander hears about it!"

We don't know exactly what the Sanhedrin tried to do about the situation down in Perea, but John soon moved away from there and started doing his baptizing in an independent territory called Decapolis, which was outside the jurisdiction of Pilate and Herod Antipas, and the Sanhedrin.

No doubt the move spelled "relief" in the leaders' minds.

But then the other shoe dropped.

Trouble on the horizon

Reports began to filter in about a new preacher—one whom John had apparently pointed to as his successor.

The news was not good. John had said some radical things about this new Man. Things like: " 'I indeed baptize you with water unto repentance, but He who is coming after me is mightier than I, whose sandals I am not worthy to carry. He will baptize you with the Holy Spirit and fire' " (Matthew 3:11).

"If that's not a reference to Malachi's Messianic prophecies, I don't know what it is," I can hear a scribe saying as he turned in the scroll to the prophecy in question: "But who can endure the day of His coming? And who can stand when He appears? For He is like a refiner's fire and like launderer's soap. He will sit as a refiner and a purifier of silver; he will purify the sons of Levi, and purge them as gold and silver, that they may offer to the LORD an offering in righteousness" (Malachi 3:2, 3). "The two of them are no doubt in cahoots," the scribe continues. "They're planting seeds in people's minds—trying to set up Messianic expectations without using the word itself."

"They're sly ones, all right," a priest replies. "They know that claiming to be the Messiah or King of Israel would be a capital offense in Pilate's eyes. So, I hear John's gone off to Decapolis, and this other fellow—they call him Joshua* I think—he's working the territory down by the Jordan, not far from Jericho."

"They call the new guy Joshua?" another priest asked.

"Yes."

"Oh, boy. That's trouble for sure."

---

*The name Jesus is an English form of Iesous, which is the Greek rendition of the Hebrew name Yeshua or Yehoshua—the name of the man we know as Joshua, who led Israel into the Promised Land after Moses died.

"What do you mean?"

"Think about it, man. This John fellow—everybody calls him a prophet—he goes over to Perea—across the Jordan. Starts dipping people in the river. Then a guy called Joshua shows up, and the prophet points to him as his successor and quotes texts about the coming of the Lord. Then both of them move across to this side of the river. Are you getting the picture yet?"

"I hadn't thought of it before—how did I miss it. It's as plain as almond blossoms in springtime. They're reenacting Israel's entrance into the Promised Land! The new leader—the one taking over from the original prophet—is even named Joshua. Just like Joshua taking over from Moses! And he starts working the territory around Jericho! I suppose next we'll start hearing about walls falling down? I wonder if we should tell Pilate?"

"Let's not get him involved! We don't want him to think we can't handle it. But we'd better be on our guard. If they start pulling any more Messianic stunts . . ."

The ticking clock

While all of this was going on, the prophetic time clock continued to tick. In the fall of Tiberius's fourteenth year (our A.D. 27), the 483rd year of Daniel's prophecy swept to a close.

Daniel 9's prophetic clock had begun ticking in the fall of 457 B.C. when the scribe Ezra led a group of Jews back to Jerusalem from Babylon, carrying a decree signed by the Persian king Artaxerxes. The decree fulfilled one aspect of Daniel's prophecy by allowing the Jews to restore and rebuild their nation in Jerusalem (see Daniel 9:25).

The prophecy called for 483 years to pass from the time of that decree until the coming of the Messiah.

It was when the 483rd year came to an end that the

Man named Joshua found His way to the Jordan and asked John to baptize Him. When Joshua came up out of the water, "the heavens were opened to Him, and He saw the Spirit of God descending like a dove and alighting upon Him" (Matthew 3:16). The arrival of the Spirit in the form of a dove signified the anointing of Joshua with the Spirit.

The term *Messiah*—which is translated into Greek as *christos* and into English as christ—means simply "anointed one."

When the 483rd year of the prophecy ended, it was time for the Messiah to begin His ministry.

The time was ripe, and the stage was set. Events in the world had all come together to make it an ideal time for the Messiah to appear.

One well-known author describes the ticking of the clock and the preparations for the coming of the Messiah in this way:

> But like the stars in the vast circuit of their appointed path, God's purposes know no haste and no delay. Through the symbols of the great darkness and the smoking furnace, God had revealed to Abraham the bondage of Israel in Egypt, and had declared that the time of their sojourning should be four hundred years. "Afterward," He said, "shall they come out with great substance." Gen. 15:14. Against that word, all the power of Pharaoh's proud empire battled in vain. On "the self-same day" appointed in the divine promise, "it came to pass, that all the hosts of the Lord went out from the land of Egypt." Ex. 12:41. So in heaven's council the hour for the coming of Christ had been determined. When the great clock of time pointed to that hour, Jesus was born in Bethlehem.
>
> "When the fullness of the time was come, God

sent forth His Son." Providence had directed the movements of nations, and the tide of human impulse and influence, until the world was ripe for the coming of the Deliverer. The nations were united under one government. One language was widely spoken, and was everywhere recognized as the language of literature. From all lands the Jews of the dispersion gathered to Jerusalem to the annual feasts. As these returned to the places of their sojourn, they could spread throughout the world the tidings of the Messiah's coming.[1]

So, the time was ripe, and the stage was set for the arrival of the Messiah.

Amazingly, God had known, more than 550 years earlier, when the prophecy of Daniel 9 was given, that the world stage would be ready for His arrival in A.D. 27. And He came, right on schedule.

But He didn't come in the way people expected.

Suddenly to His temple

That autumn of the 483rd year the Day of Atonement and the Feast of the Tabernacles passed uneventfully in Jerusalem. Neither Joshua nor John seemed inclined to make trouble for the authorities. John stayed in Decapolis, and Joshua spent most of His time down by the Jordan or up in Galilee.

The rains came, and maybe even some snow that winter. But then came spring, and Passover season. Multitudes were once again descending on Jerusalem, filling the temple courts with raucous noise as pilgrims from around the world traded their national coinage for temple money and purchased animals for sacrifice.

Suddenly the cacophony swelled to pandemonium, and then just as suddenly all was silence. What had happened?

Priests and temple rulers rushed to the scene and found Joshua, whom we'll call Jesus from now on, sitting on the temple steps, holding a little child in His lap, a whip made from sheep tethers beside Him. Down the streets, cowering in the distance, were moneychangers and sheepherders, looking on in fear, anger, and wonder—trying to figure out just what had happened and what had made them flee, leaving their treasures scattered on the floor beside their overturned tables.

" 'The Lord, whom you seek, will suddenly come to His temple,' " muttered a scribe, quoting Malachi 3:1.

"This could get serious," another replied. "Next thing we know, He'll be scrubbing the place down with fuller's soap!" (see Malachi 3:2).

They may have joked about it, but they knew that there were some hard times coming for Jerusalem, unless they could deal with this Man who was putting out all the signs that said "I'm about to claim that I'm your Messiah!"

Expectation

All of Israel was, after all, expecting the Messiah—the deliverer. The one who would come and drive out the hated Romans.

The Romans themselves had been deliverers of a sort when they had marched into the Holy Land about ninety years earlier. Israel had been a free country for about eighty years prior to that, under the Hasmonean dynasty that had driven out the hated Greek Seleucid kings. The Jews had thought their Messianic kingdom had arrived clear back then, 170 years ago (142 B.C.), when Simon, the last of the Maccabean brothers who had fought tirelessly for liberty, was installed on the throne as high priest and ruler for life.

Unfortunately, the Hasmonean rulers were all too human and proved themselves not much better on a throne than any foreign potentate. They soon fell to fighting among themselves.

When the Romans arrived on the scene, they actually brought a better sense of order to the nation than it had had under Jewish rulers. In 63 B.C., the Roman consul Pompey the Great installed a man named Antipater as procurator over much of the Jewish territory. But then the Parthians (from the area of old Persia) came marching in and captured Jerusalem. Antipater's son Herod went to Rome and won the support of the Senate, which proclaimed him king of Judea, Galilee, and Perea and sent an army large enough to drive the Parthians out. In battling the Parthians, Herod fought beside Mark Antony. It took three years, but Herod and his Roman allies finally recaptured Jerusalem in 37 B.C.

But while the Roman rulers were in some ways easier to get along with than many other foreigners, they still weren't Jews and certainly not of the lineage of Israel's most famous king, David. The prophets had promised that the line of David would rule over Israel forever, so the hope that a Jewish king would soon replace the Roman overlords continued to bubble up in Messianic expectations.

The hope floated like spring pollen in the very air of the Promised Land. True believers quoted texts from the book of Judges that pointed out that whenever God's people truly repented He would send a deliverer to drive out the foreigners and to judge and lead the people in righteousness.

John the Baptizer's message and baptism of repentance had set the stage for just that sort of thing to happen. People were repenting by the thousands, turning to God, cleaning up their acts. And the hopeful were quoting texts like Deuteronomy 33:27-29:

> The eternal God is your refuge, and underneath are the everlasting arms; *He will thrust out the en-*

emy from before you, and will say "Destroy!" Then Israel shall dwell in safety, the fountain of Jacob alone, in a land of grain and new wine; His heavens shall also drop dew. Happy are you, O Israel! Who is like you, a people saved by the LORD, the shield of your help and the sword of your majesty! *Your enemies shall submit to you,* and you shall tread down their high places.

Jesus' actions, which seemed to be obvious fulfillments of Messianic prophecies, fueled the hope. Excitement should have gripped the leaders' hearts, making them skip beats in anticipation of the great things God was about to do. But Jesus' activity only struck fear in those men's hearts. They had too much invested in the status quo to want God to break in and change things at that particular moment!

The problem was that they, along with most people, misunderstood Jesus' mission. If they had understood all the prophecies about the Anointed One, they might not have opposed Him so strongly. But their understanding of prophecy was incomplete.

Still, if they had just taken time to go back and review the story of Jesus' birth, perhaps they would have understood that He hadn't come as a sword-wielding warrior but as a lover, bent on winning men's and women's hearts.

A different king

He had been born in Bethlehem, which fulfilled the prophecy of Micah 5:2. He'd been born just over thirty years ago, right on schedule to be in the right place at the right time to live out the prophecy of Daniel 9. But He hadn't come into the world with a sword. He hadn't marshaled armies about Himself to announce His arrival and put down His enemies.

His birth had come in a humble stable, just off a road that was probably very busy with military traffic at the time, for Bethlehem is on the road from Jerusalem to Herodium—the hilltop retreat where the aging King Herod was having his tomb prepared.

Herod knew that he couldn't live much longer, but he had no intention of relinquishing his throne one second before he breathed his last. In the three years before he died, he had three of his own sons executed because he thought they were plotting to usurp his power before he was ready to lay it down.

When Herod heard that Micah 5:2 had been fulfilled with the birth in Bethlehem of "The One to be ruler in Israel" and proceeded to try to wipe out that challenger as well, Jesus' parents didn't rally the troops to defend their Son. His heavenly Father didn't send an angel to strike dead those assigned to carry out what came to be known as the slaughter of the innocents (see Matt. 2:16). Rather, an angel came and told Joseph to take his Son to Egypt for a time. In this God was setting a precedent for His Son. He would not fight for His kingdom on physical ground. The war was a war of spirits. He had come to claim the spirits of men, to liberate them from spiritual bondage. For His kingdom was not to be of this world.

He had not come to rally troops to drive out the Romans. He had come to drive out the demons.

So the priests need not have been so worried. Rather than fretting about whether this new preacher was going to cost them their freedom and their positions, they should have gone to listen to Him with pure and open hearts.

Those who did—those who really found Jesus—found something better than all their earlier Messianic expectations had led them to hope for. But it took them some time to see beyond what they expected Jesus to do for them and discover that He wasn't there to meet their expectations. He was there to exceed them.

Today He still loves to exceed people's expectations. What is it that we are expecting of Him? Are we expecting the right things? Is it possible that some of our disappointments with Jesus, some of our frustration in wondering why He hasn't returned yet, could also be based on false expectations? Or perhaps on misreading of prophecies or focusing on certain portions of the prophecies and missing other parts?

As we continue our search for clues, let's take a look at our expectations and see whether we're missing something, or perhaps expecting something Jesus never promised.

---

1. Ellen G. White, *The Desire of Ages* (Nampa, Idaho: Pacific Press® Publishing Association, 1940), 32.

CHAPTER 4

What Should We Expect From Jesus?

As we continue our search for clues about Jesus, His character, and the promises He made, we're going to jump forward about three years—skipping over the majority of His ministry on earth. Not because what He did in the meantime is unimportant. No, not by any means. There's a lot to be learned from what He did in the intervening years. Personally I've focused much of my devotional time in recent years on looking carefully at the gospel stories about Jesus. There's a lot to be learned there—even if you think you already know all the stories.

One thing I've done since late 1997 is write a brief devotional every week based on some event in Jesus' life. I send these devotionals out by e-mail to anyone who wants to receive them, so if you have e-mail and would like to receive the devotional I call "A Fresh Look at Jesus" each week, just send a message to freshlook@worldnet.att.net . Put the word *subscribe* in the subject, and I'll add you to the list. It's free!

For now, though, it's time to focus on the last year of Jesus' ministry on earth and to take a careful look at the prophecies He gave and the promises He made about His second coming.

And so we jump from Passover, A.D. 28—the time when Jesus came to Jerusalem and cleansed the temple the first time—to Passover season, A.D. 31 and the things that happened in the year leading up to Jesus' last Passover on earth.

The spring of the eighteenth year of the Roman emperor Tiberius Caesar had come to Jerusalem, and so had the pilgrims—arriving in hordes every day. Jerusalem's population always swelled at this time as faithful Jews from all over the known world came to celebrate the Passover. It was a great time for renewing old friendships and catching up on the latest news.

It was a high time—a time of celebration and joy.

And the question on almost everyone's mind was, Will that new preacher we've heard so much about be there?

"Do you think we'll get to see the new Rabbi?" young Issachar, who is attending his first Passover, asks his father. "Do you think He'll come to the Passover?"

"Of course He will," answers his father. "Every good son of Israel wants to be in Jerusalem for Passover. We'll just have to keep our eyes open—watch for any big crowds gathering. I'd sure like to see Him. They say He works miracles—even raised a man from the dead!"

As news of the new Teacher spread among the pilgrims, excitement built to a fever pitch.

But the upper classes—the rulers—still were far from enthusiastic.

They'd rather He'd stay out in the countryside, where He'd been preaching lately. If He'd just stay away at least until the crowds died down, things would go a lot smoother.

They had been keeping an uneasy eye on Him for three years now. And things had not always gone well for them. It seemed that Jesus was always growing in popularity—at their expense!

Problems at Passover

Just last year—at Passover—Jesus had healed a lame man on the Sabbath. Now, that was a clear step over the line. It was against the rules to heal on Sabbath. So they tried to help the people see that if Jesus really were a holy man, He would have more respect for their laws.

But it hadn't worked. The people took Jesus' compassion and healing miracles as evidence that He was closer to God than His law-loving opponents. Imagine that! They preferred a Man who loved people to a man who loved the law!

Back then, the crowds following Jesus had been growing every day. But then the scribes and Pharisees finally got a break! Jesus Himself started doing things that turned people away.

One day He stood up in the temple and said " 'I am the bread of life that came down from heaven' " (John 6:40), and " 'Most assuredly I say to you, unless you eat the flesh of the Son of Man and drink His blood, you have no life in you' " (John 6:53).

That was too much for most people. Soon the crowds began to dwindle. After He made a few more radical statements, almost everyone was gone. Only the faithful few disciples who had followed Jesus for most of His ministry remained with Him.

When things started going downhill for Jesus, the Jewish rulers breathed a sigh of relief. One more Messiah-pretender was about to bite the dust, and they hadn't had to involve the Romans in getting rid of Him.

Word went out on the street that the miracle worker had taken leave of His senses or that maybe all His fame was finally getting to Him and He was stressing out and going over the line into egomania.

Many people were admitting that the Pharisees had been right all along when they accused Jesus of working His miracles by the power of Beelzebub. According to John 7:20, in one confrontation, "the people answered and said,

'You have a demon!'"

"Ahh!" said the Pharisees. "YES!" said the scribes. "Finally the foolish masses are seeing through him. There will be peace in our time!" said the priests. Then, as if to fulfill their wildest dreams, Jesus gave them an excuse to get rid of Him. He blasphemed! A sin worthy of the death penalty.

What did Jesus say that could earn Him the death penalty?

Just this simple statement found in John 8:58: " 'Most assuredly, I say to you, before Abraham was, I AM.'"

That was it. That brought the house tumbling down around Jesus' shoulders. The Jews understood clearly that Jesus wasn't just claiming to have been alive 2,000 years ago when Abraham was alive. He was claiming to be God—Yahweh—the great I AM! The One whom Moses had met at the burning bush.

So, when Jesus said " 'Before Abraham was, I AM,' " that was blasphemy plain and simple in their book. And everyone knew what to do with a blasphemer. Deuteronomy 24:16 gives the instructions: "All the congregation shall certainly stone him!"

The people had actually gone so far as to pick up the rocks, ready to throw them at Him. But Jesus somehow slipped away through the crowd undetected.

He didn't disappear for long, though.

Soon reports came to the temple that Jesus had healed a man who had been born blind.

When the Pharisees confronted Him later, He told them—the most self-righteous group in the country—that if they had been blind, they would have been all right, but since they claimed to be able to see, their *sin* remained.

What an accusation to make toward people whose whole lives were devoted to avoiding sin! But Jesus said it. They needed to hear it, so He said it.

He certainly wasn't out to make "brownie points" with them.

In the ensuing weeks, Jesus said more things that offended both the Pharisees and the common people. When He openly declared " 'I am the Son of God,' " they once again tried to seize Him, but He escaped again.

This time Jesus decided to leave Jerusalem. He went down the twisting, narrow road, toward the Jordan River, past Jericho, and crossed the Jordan into Perea. Doing this was something like crossing into a different state or province. He was still in an area controlled by the Romans, but Perea and Galilee were ruled by Herod Antipas, not by the Roman procurator Pilate.

Jesus taught, preached, and healed in the region beyond the Jordan for several months, meeting the needs of the people and lifting their thoughts toward heaven.

The Jewish leaders were glad to have Him over there, out of their hair.

But then, a few months later, as the winter of Tiberius's eighteenth year began to wane and the almonds began to blossom, promising spring and Passover soon to come, Jesus received a message that brought Him back into the Pharisees' bailiwick.

The message came from His close friends Mary and Martha, who lived in Bethany—a suburb of Jerusalem. Their brother Lazarus was deathly sick, but they knew that Jesus could heal him. So they sent a messenger down the hill to find Him.

Jesus made the long climb back up to Bethany, just across the Kidron Valley from Jerusalem. But Lazarus died before He arrived. Of course, that didn't stop Jesus. He worked His greatest miracle yet—resurrecting a man who had been dead for several days.

So, in the spring of Tiberius's eighteenth year, it didn't

take long for word to reach the priests that Jesus had come back—in full strength, winning the crowds over with miraculous deeds. The leaders could see trouble on their horizon. Again!

The fickle crowds flocking to Jesus were infected with "Passover fever." Passover was the most popular of the annual feasts. More people came to Jerusalem for that event than any other, and although Passover was still a few days away, the city was already brimming with out-of-towners.

The feast commemorated the time God had delivered Israel's ancestors from domination by the great Egyptian Empire.

The increased crowds and the increased focus on deliverance from enslavement created a potentially explosive brew. The Pharisees knew they needed to deal with the situation before it got out of hand.

They called a meeting of the Sanhedrin—the group of leaders that the Romans entrusted with the day-to-day running of affairs in Jerusalem. Notice their reaction in John 11:48: "'What shall we do? For this Man works many signs. If we let Him alone like this, everyone will believe in Him, and the Romans will come and take away both our place and nation.'"

Fascinating, isn't it, when you read it? These men, these spiritual leaders, were worried. They could see the power of God working through Jesus. But it worried them rather than pleased them.

What was their problem? What were they afraid of?

Jesus threatened their place—their position of power.

Jesus brought the *power of God* to play in their world, and all they could think of was that *they* would lose *their* power!

Priestly solution

Caiaphas, the high priest who had been appointed to his office by the Romans (under the Roman procurators the office was often purchased at great expense), had the most to lose if Jesus started a rebellion. And he could see only one solution.

Kill Jesus.

Let the chips fall where they may.

By having the courage to take action now, they would save the whole nation from grief at the hands of the Romans.

Caiaphas's speech carried the day.

The plot was hatched.

Whatever it took, they would find a way to entrap Jesus and kill Him or have Him killed by the Romans. It didn't matter which. The important thing was to silence His voice and stop His miracles.

The only problem was, Jesus was wise to them. He heard about their scheming, so He left Jerusalem again. He knew His time was coming. He was ready to give His life as a sacrifice for the world. But it wasn't quite time . . . yet.

Because the Passover had not yet come.

And He was the Lamb of God to take away the sin of the world.

The only appropriate time for Him to give His life as a sacrifice would be at the Passover.

So He quietly slipped away, biding His time in a little village, until Jerusalem had become a mass of expectant pilgrims, all looking, wondering whether Jesus would come again.

Return to Jerusalem

He didn't disappoint them.

And He made sure everyone knew about His coming this time.

This Man who had so often slipped away into the wilderness to avoid the limelight; who had often told those He healed to keep quiet about it to avoid attracting too much attention, now became a part of one of the greatest publicity events ever staged. No one could miss this coming!

This time He didn't just slip quietly into the city through a side gate.

No, not this time.

This time He told His disciples to go find Him a colt—the foal of a donkey. They went away puzzled, but by the time they came back, they knew what He had in mind.

One of the great prophecies that hopeful people loved to quote when they talked about what the Messiah would do was Zechariah 9:8 and 9.

It seemed to speak directly to their need at this time, when Rome's oppressive army marched daily through their land.

Listen to God's promise and think of what it meant to His people that day when Jesus rode that little donkey into Jerusalem:

> I will camp around My house because of the army, because of him who passes by and him who returns. *No more shall an oppressor pass through them*, for now I have seen with My eyes.
> Rejoice greatly, O daughter of Zion! Shout, O daughter of Jerusalem! Behold, your King is coming to you; he is just and having salvation, lowly and riding on a donkey, a colt, the foal of a donkey (Zechariah 9:8, 9).

When the disciples brought back the colt, they knew exactly what to do. They stripped off their outer garments and made a couch on the young donkey's back, for their King to sit on while He rode into Jerusalem.

The crowds of Passover pilgrims joined in the exuberance.

They took off their cloaks and cut down palm branches and prepared the way for Jesus, just as they would for royalty. Children, the young, the old, everyone joined in the exhilarating joy of the moment, parading along, singing, shouting " 'Hosanna to the Son of David! "Blessed is He who comes in the name of the Lord!" Hosanna in the highest!' " (Matthew 21:9).

Expectations fulfilled

The excitement couldn't be contained now. The people *knew* their hopes were about to be fulfilled. Jesus was clearly the fulfillment of the Messianic prophecies they built their hopes on.

But the scribes, Pharisees, and priests remained distant, aloof, pondering their next move. It would be difficult to execute their evil designs on Jesus now, with so many people around Him.

As kingdom hopes swelled and throbbed around Jesus, He met the opposition head on, unmasking the hypocrisy of the scribes and Pharisees in public. Minute by minute it became clearer and clearer to the disciples and other faithful followers that the climax was drawing near. Soon the collaborating, traitorous scribes and Pharisees would be deposed—their cooperation with the Roman overlords ended, and Jesus (and they) would be setting up a new kingdom.

With such excitement in the city, the authorities seemed powerless to touch Jesus, even when He spoke the burden of His heart in words that only reiterated their worst fears of where His leadership was taking the nation.

After rebuking the Pharisees for their hypocrisy, He stood looking at the city He had ridden into in triumph, and spoke with tears in His voice, " 'O Jerusalem, Jerusalem, the one who kills the prophets and stones those who are sent to her! How often I wanted to gather your children together, as a hen gathers her chicks under her wings, but you were not willing! See! Your house is left to you desolate' " (Matthew 23:37, 38).

With that, Jesus left town again, passing through the Kidron Valley and up onto the Mount of Olives. He sat down there, looking back upon the city whose fate He had just mourned aloud.

But the disciples seem not to have heard, or not to have understood what He had said. As they sat with Him, looking at the city, they began to remark on how beautiful the temple was. No doubt they were thinking of the soon-coming time when, as Jesus' lieutenants, they would be in charge of the glorious city.

Jesus' response stopped them stone cold: " 'Do you not see all these things? Assuredly, I say to you, not one stone shall be left here upon another, that shall not be thrown down' " (Matthew 24:2).

A vision of the future

What could He mean by that? They knew a revolution was in the air. They expected Him to lead them in a war that would drive the Roman oppressors out. But why would the temple be destroyed? Wouldn't He defend it at all costs? What did He mean? Didn't He plan to fulfill their expectations?

Now that He had their attention, Jesus told them what they really should expect to happen in the future. His description is still being fulfilled today. And His explanation can help us answer a question that troubles many today: Why hasn't Jesus come back yet? Why hasn't He fulfilled OUR expectations?

Jesus' description of the future is found in Matthew 24.

And He pointed to three key mistakes that could lead people astray:

1. • Mistaken identities
2. • Mistaken hopes
3. • Mistaken timing

1. Mistaken identities. He predicted that there would be false christs and false prophets, who would come and lead people to false hopes. " 'Then if anyone says to you, "Look, here is the Christ!" or "There!" do not believe it. For false christs and false prophets will arise and show great signs and wonders so as to deceive, if possible, even the elect' " (Matthew 24:23, 24).

These false christs and prophets would set up hopes that Jesus was going to return sooner than He really would.

2. Mistaken hopes. In Jesus' day people were *expecting* the Messiah to do and say certain things, and it was easy for them to seize upon those prophecies that agreed with their preferred future.

So they focused on prophecies of Israel's exaltation under the Messiah without reading those portions of the passage that spoke of the need to repent and truly serve the Lord in humility, charity, and love. This led many to accept impostors who promised military victories but led the people to ignominious defeats.

The priests and Pharisees, on the other hand, didn't really want the Lord to come and disturb their peaceful, prosperous collaboration with the Romans. But if He had to come, they'd be glad for Him to suddenly come to His temple and judge the unrighteous, as Malachi promised, as long as He didn't try refining away their own self-serving actions in the fire—which was also a part of the same prophecy.

Jesus pointed out that this same sort of contentment with the status quo would make many people less-than-enthusiastic about the Second Coming. And people's hopes that the kingdom could be brought in without first enduring a time of turmoil and trial would also be disappointed.

3. Mistaken timing. At the first coming there were errors on both ends of the spectrum. False messiahs built up people's hopes before the appointed time; priests weren't ready when Jesus did appear; and Jesus predicted that at the end the same problems would occur.

False christs would prematurely proclaim the kingdom come, and others would put it off too far, as Jesus described in the parable of the householder and the robber:

> Watch therefore, for you do not know what hour your Lord is coming. But know this, that if the master of the house had known what hour the thief would come, he would have watched and not allowed his house to be broken into. Therefore, you also be ready, for the Son of Man is coming at an hour you do not expect (Matthew 24:42-44).

Jesus well understood that the signs, prophecies, omens, hopes, and expectations surrounding His return would confuse many. After all, that is what had happened with His first coming. Many had jumped the gun and proclaimed other leaders as the messiah before Jesus came. And many were not ready to receive Him when He came.

It came down to an issue of expectations. Jesus didn't meet their expectations for a messiah, and so, even when the time for the fulfillment of the Messianic prophecies arrived, most people weren't ready.

There was a lot of confusion and misinformation centered around the first coming of Jesus. And His words in Matthew 24 make it clear that we shouldn't expect it to be much different in the days leading up to His second coming.

Many today have grown weary of waiting for Jesus. They think He should have come back long ago. But could it be that they are simply victims of mistaken expectations and mistaken timing?

The old credibility question

One of the chief problems facing Christians who still believe that Jesus will return soon is the challenge to the credibility of the One who promised so long ago to return soon but who still hasn't come back.

People say, Either He didn't know what He was talking about, or He was just a plain old liar. After all, He said " 'Surely I am coming quickly' " more than 1,900 years ago.

We looked at these credibility issues in chapter 2, but at this point let's consider a few other bits of evidence, in hopes of putting this question to rest once and for all.

Remember, when Jesus said that Lazarus's illness would not *end* in death, He was right, even though it seemed for a time that He had been wrong. Jesus' timing was just a bit different from His friends'.

The same sort of thing happened when Jairus, the synagogue ruler, asked Jesus to come and heal his daughter. While Jesus was still on the way, word came that the girl had died, but Jesus said " 'Do not be afraid; only believe, and she will be made well' " (Luke 8:50). Out of disappointment and death sprang new life and joy. When Jesus finally arrived on the scene, He woke the girl from the sleep of death. Though Jesus seemed to be late in both cases, in the end Jesus delivered something even better than what people had expected.

Before He died, Jesus promised to rise again. His disciples went through a terrible time of disappointment, disillusionment, and confusion because they didn't listen carefully and accept His words. But that didn't stop Him from rising. It didn't stop Him from bringing about something better than they had expected—exceeding their expectations.

When Jesus ascended to heaven, He promised to send the Holy Spirit. It didn't happen right away, but when the disciples got together and united their spirits and their prayers, the Spirit descended, bringing power and joy they never could have anticipated.

So there's no reason to doubt that Jesus will fulfill His promises. Let's put away the question of credibility and take a closer look at our expectations in comparison to what Jesus really promised. Because while there is no reason to doubt that Jesus will keep His word, there is reason to doubt that the fulfillment will come about in just the way, or at just the time, most people expect it to.

Expectations, expectations

Today we see all kinds of expectations being set up by Christian teachers. A best-selling set of fictional books has ridden the crest of excitement over the turn of the millennium. The authors, Tim LaHaye and Jerry B. Jenkins, have certain expectations about what will happen in Israel and other places just before Jesus comes, and they play these hopes out on a convincing story canvas. But are they right? Should we be expecting Russia to launch all-out war against tiny Israel any day now? And should we anticipate that the Lord will act, striking down the MIG-29s and long-range bombers in midflight?

Other Christians preach that the Moslem mosque on the temple mount in Jerusalem will have to be torn down and a new Jewish temple built there before the Second Coming can occur. But are their expectations truly in line with biblical prophecy?

Recently a group calling themselves the "Concerned Christians" planned to start a gunfight with Israeli police so that they, the "Concerned Christians," could all die in Jerusalem. They thought this would hasten the return of Jesus.

Some Christians focus in on certain portions of Matthew 24 and proclaim that there have to be more famines, pestilence, and wars before Jesus can return. Some of them, in 1999, are looking forward with eager anticipation toward January 1, 2000, when they expect the much-publicized Y2K computer glitch to throw the world into a tailspin of turmoil that will finally bring on the consummation.

But are these the things we should be waiting for? Are these the ultimate fulfillments that Jesus wants us to be looking for with earnest longing? Is it the lack of these things that has prevented Him from returning so far?

I hardly think so.

There are certain things that Jesus said would happen before His return. Most of the signs people tend to focus on—such as wars, famines, pestilence, earthquakes—are included in His list of things that are only "the beginning of sorrows":

> And you will hear of wars and rumors of wars. See that you are not troubled; for all these things must come to pass, but the end is not yet. For nation will rise against nation, and kingdom against kingdom. And there will be famines, pestilence, and earthquakes in various places. *All these are the beginning of sorrows* (Matthew 24:6-8).

But one thing He predicted really intrigues me, because it's the thing He *actually* predicted would come just before the end. Do you know what it is? Here it is in Matthew 24:14: " 'And this gospel of the kingdom will be preached in all the world as a witness to all the nations, and then the end will come.' "

What a fantastic promise. The Good News will go to everyone!

That's something you and I can get involved in.

But He also mentioned some other things that will happen before that final sign is fulfilled. Many prophetic interpreters have failed to notice these things. Few have put all the pieces together to discover all that Jesus predicted and the things that are happening in our world right now to set the stage for His second coming.

We'll take a look at these things in upcoming chapters, but first let's remind ourselves where we are on the Bible's prophetic calendar.

CHAPTER 5

Is Time Running Out?

Where are we on the prophetic calendar?

It has been popular through the years to picture a clock with its hands nearing midnight.

But are we really living in the last days of earth's history? Should we interpret everything we see around us as signs that Jesus is going to return soon?

Well, of course, if you ask some Christians, they'll be glad to tell you that *Yes*, there are signs all around us pointing to the soon return of Jesus.

They'll get out their newspaper and show you articles about wars and rumors of wars. And of course every war and rumor of war is another tick mark they can check off on their list of evidences that the end of the world is drawing nigh. If there's an earthquake in southern California or over in Turkey, they'll point to it and say—"See! Another sign that Jesus is coming soon!"

I'll never forget one dear little lady I used to visit quite regularly when I was a young intern pastor. If I'd go to visit her in the summertime and it was an especially hot day, she'd say "Oh, isn't the weather hot—just one more sign that the Lord's coming soon!" And if I'd visit her on a cold day in the winter—well, you know what she'd say.

In a way, I suppose, that kind of thinking is good. The

dear lady was anxious for the return of her best Friend, Jesus. And she wanted to see her husband again—he'd died a number of years earlier. She was just looking for any possible evidence that the day would be soon. And she was thinking of some of the things Jesus said would happen before that day. They're found in Matthew 24:6, 7:

> And you will hear of wars and rumors of wars. See that you are not troubled; for all these things must come to pass, but the end is not yet. For nation will rise against nation, and kingdom against kingdom. And there will be famines, pestilence, and earthquakes in various places.

Jesus spoke of these disturbances coming upon the earth before the end, and my friend saw anything unusual that happened as one of the signs of His return.

But there is a little danger in seeing *everything* as a sign of Jesus' soon return. We can get burned out on hope, after a while, and become disillusioned—and eventually lose all hope.

Is Jesus just waiting for enough famines, earthquakes, and wars on earth? Or is there something else we should be looking for? What *is* Jesus waiting for?

Enough disasters?

I did a little research on the Internet recently, and do you know what I figured out?

I figured out that if that's what Jesus is waiting for, He should have returned in 1943.

"Nineteen forty-three?" you ask. "I've heard that many people expected Him in 1843, but never 1943! What's so significant about that year?"

Well, a lot, really. It was the middle of World War II. There were certainly plenty of wars and rumors of wars.

And of course where there's war, there's always famine and disease. But do you know what really caught my eye?

I visited the homepage of the National Earthquake Information Center. They have a list of the number of major earthquakes per year for the last hundred years. And do you know what year had the most major earthquakes—by far—of any year in the twentieth century?

You guessed it. Nineteen forty-three. There were forty-one earthquakes over 7.0 magnitude. By contrast, the highest number in the 1990s was twenty-five.

So, if Jesus was just waiting for plenty of earthquakes, war, famines, etc., He should have come in 1943, don't you think?

But could it be that Jesus is waiting for something else? That He has His own timetable?

Prognosticators unlimited

There have been a lot of attempts, through the years, to pinpoint a date for the Second Coming.

About 1,600 years ago, a rumor began to make the rounds in Constantinople. Nobody knows who started the rumor, but it certainly didn't have any biblical foundation.

The story, as related in the rumor, was that the apostle Peter had made a deal with the devil, whereby Christianity would be allowed to exist for 365 years. Many Christians at that time believed that Jesus had ascended to heaven and founded Christianity in A.D. 33.

Of course 33 plus 365 is 398. Then, in 398, Constantinople was shaken to its foundations by a devastating earthquake.

The disaster, combined with the rumor, led to a panic. People assumed that Jesus planned to make good on Peter's deal by coming back at the end of the 365 years to deal with the devil once and for all. According to the Christian scholar

Augustine, who was alive at that time, "Everyone, almost with violence, demanded baptism from whom he could. Not only in church, but also in their homes and through the streets and squares there was a cry for the saving sacrament, that they might escape wrath."[1]

What a story! It seems some people just needed to be scared into the kingdom!

But 398 was not the end of the world. Neither was it the last attempt to predict when the end would come.

Here's another fascinating story that historians have just recently uncovered:

Back in Augustine's days, Christians commonly believed that the earth had been created 5,500 years before the birth of Christ. And church documents were dated "Anno Mundi." That is—by the number of years since Creation.

Well, as the year we'd call A.D. 500 approached, the Anno Mundi calendar approached the year 6000.

Now, you're no doubt aware that many people today think that the world will be 6,000 years old in the year 2000. And many expect Jesus to return around 2000 to celebrate the six-thousandth year since Creation.

Many Christian organizations have capitalized on interest in the turn of the millennium. Pope John Paul II has declared A.D. 2000 a year of jubilee. There will be celebrations all over the world.

But as Anno Mundi 6000 approached, it evoked fear, not celebration.

In fact, church leaders were so fearful of how the masses would react to the coming of the year 6000, they changed the way they numbered the years!

Before the fateful year 6000 was reached, they adopted a new chronology! They changed the year of Creation! They decided that Creation had occurred 5,200 years before the birth of Jesus, not 5,500. By doing that, they put off the day of reckoning by 300 years![2]

Three hundred years later, when the numbers started approaching 6,000 again, church authorities adopted a new numbering system: the B.C.-A.D. system we still use today! They just didn't want to face the year 6000, for fear that that people would think the world was about to end.

The switch to the B.C.-A.D. numbering system bought the church another two centuries of peace. But soon there was a bit of a crisis as the year 1000 approached.

Fortunately most people at that time were not aware of the numbering of the years. Most people were illiterate, and those who did count the years employed a wide variety of numbering systems. There was some end-of-the-world excitement as 1000 approached, but the year 1033 actually evoked more interest. Massive throngs of pilgrims descended on Jerusalem in hopes of being at the Mount of Olives when Jesus descended from heaven.

Well, as we enter the third millennium, it's been more than 1,600 years since the excitement of 398 and a thousand years from the turn to 1000. And along the way Christians have proposed a multitude of dates for the return of Jesus.

What's fascinating is that since the year 1000 people's attitudes have shifted 180 degrees. Before 1000, church leaders did everything they could to keep people from getting excited about the end of the world. They changed the calendar twice to avoid exciting the masses.

But in the past 1,000 years, many Bible scholars have gone looking for dates that were close at hand, in order to arouse interest.

As the year 1260 approached, a man named Joachim floated the theory that since there had been forty-two generations from Adam to Christ, there would also be forty-two from Christ to the consummation. Assigning thirty years to a generation, he concluded that a new age would dawn around 1260. When that didn't happen, a group founded in 1260 began to point to the year 1300 as the final year.

Other dates that various Bible students set for the end include 1500, 1656, 1843, 1844, 1901, 1914, 1964, 1975, 1984, 1988, 1994, 1996, 1998, 2000, 2001, and 2007. As the year 2000 approached, the fervor for date setting increased.

What about it?

Should we be excited about the year 2000—or perhaps 2001? You've probably heard the reasoning some people use: They believe that earth was created about 4,000 years before the birth of Jesus, and adding 2,000 years brings us to the end of six millennia.

Many Christians hope that the seventh millennium will be a "Sabbath rest" for the earth—the thousand years of peace described in Revelation 20.

It seems that many Christians now assume that Creation occurred about 4,000 years before Christ's birth, rather than 5,500 years as earlier Christians believed. They base this on Ussher's chronology, which set the date of Creation as October 22, 4004 B.C. Many older Bibles have that date in their marginal references as the date of Creation.

I'm not sure why those who are emphasizing the turn of the millennium as the date of the end of the world miss the point that the six-thousandth year since Ussher's Creation date already passed in 1997. Perhaps it's just more interesting to focus on big, round numbers like 2000.

Whatever the reason, the failure of so many earlier expectations that were based on chronological reckoning doesn't bode well for those who think the turn of the millennium means Jesus *has* to return either in 2000 or 2001.

Jesus made it clear that no one knows the exact date of His return. Here is His own testimony in Matthew 24:36: " 'But of that day and hour no one knows, not even the angels of heaven, but My Father only' " (Matthew 24:36).

Of course some people counter that by saying "We're not predicting the day or the hour—but no one said we can't predict the *year!*"

But the reckoning they use to point to the year 2000 isn't any more reliable than the reckoning used to set a multitude of other years.

Longest prophecy

As close as I can tell, the last time-oriented prophecy in the Bible pointed to a year more than 150 years in our past. That was the prophecy that ignited the Millerite excitement centered around the years 1843 and 1844.

It's found in Daniel 8 and is closely related to one of the most amazing time prophecies in the entire Bible—the prophecy in Daniel 9:24-27 that predicted the years of both Jesus' baptism and His crucifixion.

In the early 1800s, William Miller, who had been a captain in the U.S. forces that fought the British in the War of 1812, began studying Daniel's prophecies.

He focused especially on Daniel 9:24-27 and this prophecy found in Daniel 8:14: "And he said to me, 'For two thousand three hundred days; then the sanctuary shall be cleansed.' "

Miller noticed that these two prophecies seemed to have the same starting point, because the shorter prophecy of Daniel 9 came to Daniel while he was puzzling and praying about the meaning of the prophecy given to him in chapter 8. Furthermore, he noticed that a literal translation of Daniel 9:24 could indicate that the seventy weeks mentioned there were "cut off" from something.

It seemed logical to him that these seventy weeks, which pointed forward to the ministry and crucifixion of Jesus, must have been a portion of the longer prophecy that Daniel had been praying about.

Miller soon came to some startling conclusions. It seemed to him that the Bible's longest time prophecy was about to reach its end—in the year 1843. And he believed it pointed to the date for Jesus' second coming!

The prophecy pointed to the time when "the sanctuary shall be cleansed," and Miller assumed that meant the earth itself would be cleansed by the fire of the Second Coming.

When 1843 passed uneventfully, Miller figured he must have been wrong, but some of his followers were not easily discouraged. They figured out that they probably had originally been off by a year—that because the calendar has no zero year all calculations between B.C. and A.D. have to have a year added to them—so the prophecy actually pointed to 1844.

One preacher even went so far as to predict that Jesus would return on October 22, 1844, because he believed that that was the date of the annual Day of Atonement in the Jewish calendar. Miller wasn't easily persuaded at first, but later he seems to have actually added some fervor to the expectation.

That date, October 22, rang a bell with Miller, because Ussher's chronology stated that God had begun to create the earth on October 22, 4004 B.C. But Miller didn't buy all of Ussher's reckoning. He added a year here and a century there, and came to the conclusion that the six-thousandth year since Creation would end on October 22, 1844!

When the 6000-year reckoning seemed to coincide with the new calculations based on Daniel 8 and 9, it made many people feel very sure that the world would end on that day.

But it didn't.

The Bible's longest time prophecy came to an end without bringing the end of the world. William Miller and many of his followers became discouraged. They assumed that they had been altogether wrong in their calculations and gave up hope that Jesus would return anytime soon.

But other Bible students continued to study the prophecies and came to the conclusion that Daniel 8:14 had never been intended to point toward the date for the end of the world. Rather, it pointed to the time when the final events of earth's history would begin. This involved Jesus' ministry in heaven, in preparation for His second coming.

The time is ripe

What the longest prophecy actually pointed out was that the time was ripe—not fulfilled. Jesus could come back very soon. But we still don't have a specific date to fix our hopes on. Jesus told us we wouldn't.

So, what about now? The longest time prophecy expired over 150 years ago, and since that date we've been living in the "time is ripe" period. Is there any reason to believe that this time of waiting won't go on for another 150 or more years? Or how about for another millennium?

There is no time prophecy that says it won't happen that way.

But there are some other pieces of evidence that I think we need to consider before we jump to any conclusions about how much longer it could be before Jesus returns.

The October 1998 issue of *National Geographic* magazine included a fascinating map. It deals with population growth on our planet. Putting the information on that map together with statistics from the United Nations, I discovered some astounding things that I think we need to consider as we think about our future.

Do you have any idea what the population of the world was when Jesus was born? According to the best figures available, there were about 300 million people alive at that time. About the combined populations of the United States and Canada today. A thousand years later, at the turn of the first millennium, the earth's population had grown by only about ten million, to 310 million.

But in the thousand years since then, we've gone up to nearly six billion! That's a phenomenal growth rate, and most of the increase has occurred in just the past one or two centuries.

The *National Geographic* map included some charts, predicting how population might grow in the next 150 years. If the birth rate in undeveloped areas doesn't decline drastically, there could be as many as 27 billion people on earth by A.D. 2150! That's scary. But it gets scarier yet if you project population growth over the past millennium out for another thousand years. If growth in the next millennium is anything like it was in the one past, the year A.D. 3000 would find 116 billion people struggling to find a foothold on our planet.

No one is sure just how many people earth can support, but most authorities agree that we're about maxed out already. Simply put, things just *can't* go on as they are for too much longer. Something has to change drastically.

You know, after looking at those statistics and considering the fact that the areas of most rapid growth are in parts of the world least equipped to feed more mouths, I began to wonder just how long Jesus could possibly wait to come back and put an end to human suffering. I went to my Bible and reread Matthew 9:36-38 with this in mind:

> But when He saw the multitudes, He was moved
> with compassion for them, because they were weary
> and scattered, like sheep having no shepherd. Then
> He said to His disciples, "The harvest truly is plenti-
> ful, but the laborers are few. Therefore pray the Lord
> of the harvest to send out laborers into His harvest."

Compassion and the harvest

Jesus felt compassion for the multitudes in His day. Think how much more He must feel the needs of the suffering billions today.

It was a long time ago that Jesus promised to come back. I can't help but believe that He really wants to fulfill that promise. And I can't help but believe that His compassionate concern for the masses gives Him additional reason to want to do it soon.

I believe that right now He's appealing to us—on the same basis that He spoke to His disciples when He was on earth: Look around you at the suffering multitudes. The harvest of earth is ready. So pray that God will soon send harvesters out to reap.

And there's another aspect of this population issue that I had never thought of until just recently. When Jesus looked around at the masses, He seemed pleased at how plentiful the potential harvest was: thousands of souls just waiting to be ushered into the kingdom.

When God created the earth and our first ancestors, He told them to be fruitful and multiply and fill the earth. When He set life in motion, He intended that there would be millions and billions of souls here—beings created in His own image—people He could have for friends.

Could it be that He has been waiting and watching all these years for a time when the earth would produce its highest possible yield of souls for salvation? Has He waited this long so there will be more souls to populate heaven?

You and I certainly shouldn't complain that He didn't return 150 years ago. We should be glad He waited until we had a chance to live and be a part of His eternal kingdom.

There is another part of Jesus' prophecy that I believe ties in closely with this.

After Jesus spoke of wars, pestilence, earthquakes, and

famines, He assured us that these were only " 'the beginning of sorrows,' " not true signs of the imminent end (see Matthew 24:8). He went on to tell of a time when Christians would be persecuted for their faith, and many false prophets would arise, lawlessness would abound, and as a result most people's love would grow cold and they would deny their former faith.

He was describing a time of the ripening of earth's harvest of souls. A time of summer heat, as it were, that ripens both the wheat and the tares (see the parable of the wheat and tares in Matthew 13:24-30). A time of persecution that serves as a furnace to separate the gold from the dross, as described in Malachi 3:3.

But amidst all this description of trials and denials, Jesus planted one ray of hope for us to cling to. " 'And this gospel of the kingdom will be preached in all the world as a witness to all the nations, and then the end will come' " (Matthew 24:14).

Notice that it is at this time that the gospel finally goes to all the world. It's a time of marvelous opportunity for God to reach the maximum number of people possible with the good news about Himself.

The harvest is plentiful, the laborers are few, He said. But when the laborers have gone out to all the world and spread the message of the kingdom, then the end will finally come!

The two issues are tied together—the issue of the multiplied humanity, multiplied suffering and Jesus' concern for His children, and the time when the gospel can be spread to all the world.

There is a fantastic ray of hope, a spark of joy that can be set alight amidst all the suffering and potential disaster that threatens our world. For it is in this time, when it seems impossible for life to go on much longer, that the world has received another gift.

It is in this age, for the first time in history, that the whole world is tied together with lines of communication and transportation that make it possible for Matthew 24:14 to be fulfilled with blinding speed.

Now is a time when all the world can come to know about their Savior Jesus.

It's also a time for a consummation of another type.

Ever since Adam and Eve first sinned, people have been trying to serve as their own savior. They've tried a multitude of means to make the world a safe and prosperous place.

All means apart from God have, of course, failed. But God has let us keep trying new means, new technologies.

How long will He allow this to continue?

What is Jesus really waiting for?

---

1. Augustine, cited in Damian Thompson, *The End of Time* (Hanover and London: New England Press, 1966), 30.
2. Thompson, 31.

CHAPTER 6

What Is Jesus Waiting For?

In my 1994 book *The Orion Conspiracy*, I developed an end-time scenario, based in part on prophecies found in the book of Revelation, in which the United States tries to establish world peace through use of its superior military technology. The scenario drew on information I've received about futuristic weapons that are being developed right now. I pictured a sort of New World Order where space-based weapons would be called into action to strike fear into the hearts of any group that might be fanning old grudges into warlike flames. Fire would literally rain down from heaven in an attempt to enforce world peace. To some it seemed an unlikely scenario.

Then in 1999 NATO, led by US fighters, bombers, and cruise missiles, launched an air campaign against Yugoslavia in hopes of stopping the ethnic infighting going on in Kosovo. Fire rained down from heaven for more than two months, finally forcing Serbian troops to withdraw from Kosovo.

Will there be peace at last in Kosovo? Can anyone say for sure? My history books tell me that there was a major battle between Moslems and Christians there in 1389 and that the fighting has been going on ever since. Can the U.S. or any other power bring about world peace and harmony through force?

It is interesting to note that while the world's top military powers have been fully engaged in the Kosovo problem, two other erstwhile enemies, India and Pakistan, have begun trading bombs and grenades and shaking their nuclear fists at one another in a fight over a disputed portion of Kashmir. And North and South Korea are sinking ships as they fight over disputed fishing grounds.

The world is beginning to look like a school playground where all the teachers are trying to break up a fight between perennial troublemakers at one end, and the bullies have congregated at the other end to pick on whomever they can, while the only people with enough strength to stop them are looking the other way.

History has witnessed a multitude of plans for making the world a peaceful and safe place to live. Nearly two thousand four hundred years ago the Greek philosopher Plato penned his dialogue *The Republic*, proposing an ideal system of government that would provide justice and peace for the world, but no one has ever been able to create a truly just way of government.

Perhaps the closest thing to genuine world peace that's ever been achieved was the Pax Romana of the first two centuries A.D. During that time the Roman Empire was strong enough to subdue any group that would try to start a war. But there wasn't true peace during that time. In Palestine alone, there were two major revolts by the Jews.

And Christian history testifies that even though it may have been a time of overall peace, it certainly was not a time of justice. Thousands of Christians were martyred for their faith during those years, as part of the government's plan for assuring that nothing would disturb the "peace."

And, of course, Rome really controlled only a small part of the world. So even if the peace had been genuine, it wouldn't have been world peace.

Still, people have continued to dream of ways that humanity can solve all of its problems and create a world full of contented, peace-loving citizens who will cooperate. In the sixteenth century, Sir Thomas More described such a place in his book *Utopia*. The name of the book expresses the level of likelihood its plan could ever be worked out. *Utopia* is Greek for nowhere.

Twentieth-century writers including Aldous Huxley in *Brave New World* and George Orwell in *1984* have tended to pick up Plato's ideas about a highly controlled society and paint them in dark colors, emphasizing humankind's propensity for control that robs us of the very individuality that makes us human.

The experiences of two world wars and the atrocities committed by domineering Nazi and communist governments have demonstrated the folly of many human plans for creating a perfect world. Hitler and Stalin both promised that after a time of war, they would lead the world into an enduring time of peace and prosperity. Even Pol Pot, whose barbaric leadership caused the death of nearly a third of his fellow Cambodians, claimed his repressive methods were for the good of the people.

The use of force has never led to a truly lasting peace, and it never will.

Lasting peace cannot be brought about by force.

The only thing that will permanently dissolve the tensions in Bosnia, Kosovo, Belfast, Iraq, the Gaza Strip, Rwanda, or on the streets of Los Angeles for that matter, is a change of heart; a change of spirit; a change of attitude; a moving away from resentment, grudges, and revenge; and a movement toward reconciliation, forgetting, and forgiving.

A movement toward the principles of the gospel, in other words.

A movement toward the principles that Jesus said needed to be proclaimed to all the world before His second coming.

Why does the gospel need to go to all the world?

It's a puzzling question, really, if you look at it carefully. Why did Jesus set this up as one thing we should expect to happen before He returned?

One explanation I've heard is that everyone in the world needs to be given a chance to hear the message, so that each and every individual can either accept or reject Jesus personally.

That's a nice sounding answer, unless you ask the question: What about all the people who died before the gospel reached the whole world? What about people who are dying in India's thousands of villages right now, where the gospel has never been preached? What about the 200,000 people who starved to death in North Korea's end-of-the-millennium famine? They had been raised and educated in a nation cut off from the rest of the world, where it is basically illegal to believe in any god. What chance did they have to hear the gospel preached?

So, if people have been dying all through the centuries without hearing the gospel, why does it have to go to all the world before Jesus returns?

It seems to me that it has something to do with the overall plan of salvation.

There are many plans of salvation for our world.

Buddha proposed one in which we save ourselves through right views, right mindfulness, right conduct, and several other righteous attitudes and actions.

The Hindus have a way of salvation based on surrender of our individuality and absorption into the universal spirit.

Islam teaches that one can earn a ticket to Paradise by dying in a holy war.

Science-fiction writers are always proposing new visions of a prosperous future based on human efforts and intelligence. Gene Roddenberry's idealized world where all of earth's nations will be united into a government called The Federation continues to get a lot of air time in Star Trek series and reruns. And Arthur C. Clarke, author of *2001: A Space Odyssey* recently checked in with *3001, The Final Odyssey*. In this millennium-later sequel to his bestseller, Clarke pictures a world where humankind has literally risen above most of its problems by building four huge towers that allow the elite of society to live in a carefully-controlled environment somewhere above the stratosphere and to go from planet to planet as easily as we continent-hop today.

Serious scientists also have their visions of humanly engineered paradises. One of the most intriguing is one I found described on the Internet. In an interesting commingling of science fact and science fiction, Arthur C. Clarke has placed his seal of approval on one scientist's proposal for ensuring humankind's salvation through colonizing the whole universe. Marshall T. Savage describes this plan in his book *The Millennial Project: Colonizing the Galaxy in Eight Easy Steps*. The book was originally published in 1993 by a small publisher, but when it was picked up by a major publishing house, Clarke got on the bandwagon and wrote a new introduction for the 1994 edition.

The Millennial Project paints a glorious picture of human salvation through development of human potential. The author expresses his vision of the future in a dreamscape that almost makes you think we could solve all our problems on our own and make not just the world, but the whole universe, a better place to live. Listen to his dream:

> We now have the capacity, economically and technically, to leave this planet and begin the infinite task of enlivening the universe. We can accomplish our ends in eight easy steps: First, we will lay the Foun-

dation, uniting ourselves around the green banner of Cosmic destiny. Then we will grow a crystalline city, floating on the waves of the sea. With power from the ocean we will launch ourselves into space, propelled aloft by a rainbow-hued array of lasers. In orbit above the Earth, we will inflate gleaming golden bubbles to shelter our new generation of space dwelling people. On the face of the Moon, we will cap the craters with glistening domes, each sheltering a green oasis of life. Mars will be transformed into a glorious gem of blue oceans and swirling white clouds, vibrant and alive as Gaia herself. Among the asteroids we will strew a spreading ring-cloud of billions of billions of bubbles of life, shimmering like a galaxy of golden sparks. Finally in the latter half of the Millennium, space arks will carry human colonists across the interstellar gulfs to inseminate new worlds with the chartreuse elixir of Life. By Millennium's end the night sky will twinkle with a handful of emerald stars— the initial scattering of our celestial seeds. . . . Within a thousand millennia, the whole majestic pinwheel of the Milky Way, will be saturated with the lush aquamarine light of a hundred billion living suns. We will have created a living galaxy—seed of a living universe.[1]

Sounds wonderful, doesn't it?

As a scientist, Marshall T. Savage believes it's doable. As a futurist and science-fiction writer, Arthur C. Clarke agrees.

But there's a major problem. A major flaw. A gigantic fly in the ointment. It's the same fly that's spoiled all of humankind's salves for all of the centuries since Adam first pointed his finger at Eve and said "she's the cause of all my problems!"

The question Savage and Clarke fail to answer is: How do we get all of humanity to unite around the "green banner of Cosmic destiny?" How can we get all of humanity to unite around anything?

It's never happened yet, and it never will happen.

But that doesn't mean people will quit trying to find ways by which we can save ourselves.

The idea that we can save ourselves through our own good works, or our own intelligence, lies at the root of every religion and virtually every philosophy except Christianity.

Saving ourselves

Everything that Satan has put forth as an alternative method of salvation involves humans saving themselves.

Because the root sin that led Satan to be cast out of heaven was pride. He used pride to get Eve—"You will be like God!" he promised. You'll have all the power you need, all to yourself. You won't need God anymore!

Satan continues to put forth that lie in myriad forms. And God lets him do it. Because as part of the plan of salvation, God has chosen to let us humans have our own way for as long as it takes for us to finally figure out that we really can't save ourselves.

No human plan for salvation will ever work; simply because humanity is all too human. Fallen human nature is crippled by greed and grudges, to mention only two of our fatal flaws. And the only genuine antidote is the gospel.

But apparently we haven't yet had a chance to try all of our plans.

Do you see what I'm saying?

Ever since Adam and Eve first succumbed to Satan's alternate plan for their happiness and salvation, our earth has been a proving ground for every imagination of Lucifer and his legions.

The book of Job clearly pictures the contest that is going on for human loyalty. Ever since the day Adam surrendered his sovereignty over earth to him, Satan has been prowling about our planet, wreaking havoc and planting plans of evil genius in the minds of receptive humans.

But in Job he met a man whose loyalty he couldn't woo. It certainly wasn't for lack of trying. But after he had tried for a while, he was summoned to heaven for one of the periodic counsels that he was still invited to in spite of his rebellion. God knew what Satan had been up to, but He asked the question anyhow: "Have you had a look at My servant Job—have you noticed that he is blameless and upright, and that he fears me and doesn't give any heed when you come around?" (Job 1:8, loose paraphrase).

You're no doubt familiar with the rest of the story. Satan responded by challenging God—"Your friend Job wouldn't be so loyal if You didn't protect him from me all the time. Let me at him—just let me mess with his life a little, and then see how steadfast he is!"

And God let Satan have his little experiment. Much to Job's distress and discomfort, God let Satan demonstrate just what he'd like to do to everyone on earth if God would just get out of the way. The tragedy, pain, and suffering that ensued stand as a warning to anyone who wants to give Satan's way a try.

The book of Job opens the curtains and reveals what is going on behind the scenes in our world and in our universe. When Shakespeare penned the words "all the world's a stage," he didn't miss the truth by far.

Satan has used this stage to try a multitude of experiments, but we aren't always given the privilege of peeking behind the curtain to discover that he's the one behind it. People blame Adolph Hitler for the deaths of the six million Jews slain in the Holocaust. But who gave Hitler the ideas that led to the slaughter? If we could see behind the scenes, we'd see Satan whispering in the Führer's ear.

Mao Tse-tung's "Great Leap Forward" gets blamed for causing twenty million Chinese to starve to death in the late 1950s, and those who were tortured and imprisoned in the 1960s blame Mao's "Cultural Revolution." But was Mao the originator of these human plans for creating a perfect society in China? No. Behind him we can see the same spirit that caused the "cultural revolution" in heaven that led to Satan and his angels being cast out. It's the spirit of pride. The spirit that says "We can solve our own problems without the grace of God. We can do it better our way."

The same drama has been played out again and again on the stage—with different players, a slightly different plot, but always the same theme. Man's attempt to save himself without God's help.

The Tower of Babel and the French Revolution are the same story, played out by different actors with different props. In one it is bricks and bitumen that create a physical tower to deliver people from God's power. In the other, people build a tower of reason to escape from God.

As the story plays over and over again, it's almost as if Satan is being given the chance to try every plot permutation imaginable. But why? Wouldn't once through have been enough?

If you're a parent or a teacher, I think you understand why once through is not enough. Maybe you've read some of those moral stories that parents read to children—the ones that end "and after that Bobby never told a lie again."

I used to believe those story endings. But then I had children of my own.

It's a rare child, or adult, who can learn all the lessons he or she needs from one experience. Most of us have to learn the same lesson over and over again, through different circumstances.

We like to try things different ways. If at first we don't succeed, we try, try again.

If the world is a stage where Satan is being allowed to try out different strategies while the rest of the universe looks on, trying to judge whether Satan's way or God's is best, what would have happened if God had cut the experiment short a few years after Eden? Satan still could have appealed to the universe's court of opinion, saying "But God didn't let me try this" and "He never gave me a chance to try that."

The only reason sin has been allowed to rule in this world for so long is that God wants to get rid of it once and for all. He has chosen to let it run its full course. He's chosen to let Satan work through a multitude of leaders with myriad plans—just so the universe can see once and for all that all plans apart from God are doomed to failure.

Why the whole world?

But how does this answer the question "Why does the gospel have to go to all the world?"

Perhaps it isn't a complete answer, but here's what I'd suggest: Could it be that Jesus has been waiting for our era, when humanity would develop marvelous new technologies and scientific skill, as part of His plan to let Satan try all his plans before bringing sin's reign to a sudden, screeching halt?

In other words, could it be that God has actually been waiting for our modern scientific age in order to give us the best possible opportunity to work out our problems all on our own?

Today's electronic technology allows us to communicate instantly with people anywhere on earth. Satellites launched in the late 1990s have made our world a place where cell phones are never "out of range." A person standing at the South Pole can now dial a number and be instantly connected with a friend at the North Pole, or in the middle of the Sahara Desert.

Meanwhile, Internet technology has made the latest, breaking news instantly available. You no longer have to wait a quarter hour for CNN Headline News to get back to the top stories. On CNN's Website, you can read the story you want, when you want.

And with more and more people hooked up to e-mail, any message you want to distribute can be launched into a thousand channels at once. Recent computer viruses such as the one called Melissa have demonstrated that computers can spread messages to millions of recipients worldwide even without human participation.

With this level of communication sophistication available to us, surely we humans ought to be able to work out all our differences and solve the world's problems, wouldn't you think? Especially when you consider that there are more creative thinkers alive today than ever before.

If an e-mail won't do, then try a phone call. And if you need more people involved in the negotiations, try video conferencing over the Internet, so everyone can see and talk to the other participants in real time. If that level of communication doesn't solve the problem, then there's still good old air travel. Within a day, or two at the most, you can gather all the necessary participants together in a conference room at a five-star resort where they can be wined and dined until they arrive at some sort of amicable plan for resolving the problem peacefully.

Former US President George Bush was fond of speaking of the "New World Order." He spoke of it as a place where we can finally achieve our age-old dream of world peace and prosperity.

But any plan for solving the world's problems, whether by a New World Order or simply through new technologies, is sure to fall as flat as every other scheme in history. Humanity, apart from the perfecting influence of God's Spirit, is simply and completely incapable of solving its problems. Old grudges will continue to spark conflicts. Greed and the quest for absolute power will always corrupt leaders who are not fully controlled by the Holy Spirit.

The gospel of Jesus Christ is the only solution to these problems. The gospel of forgiveness and selflessness is the only influence that has the power to transform human beings into people who can live with each other without conflict.

Short of a total conversion of the whole human race to perfect, Spirit-led Christians, the world's problems will never be solved.

And God will never force conversion on anyone.

That's why the Second Coming is the only real solution. At that time, only those who have truly and fully surrendered to the Lord will be left alive. And as a result, humans will finally be able to live together in peace and harmony.

The Bible makes it clear that the only full and final solution to our world's problems is the Second Coming.

So, back to the question: What is Jesus waiting for?

Could it be that He promised that the gospel would go to all the world before His return precisely because He knew He would wait for this age when it finally is possible to spread a message literally to the whole world?

He's not going to continue to let Satan try out new plans for all of eternity. He has to draw a line somewhere and say "Enough is enough."

Could it be that the line is drawn at the point where we have developed enough technology to be given one last chance to solve all our problems through worldwide communication?

Is now the time when the gospel will go to all the world?

If so, how will it be accomplished? Is a satellite broadcast that is available everywhere at once enough? Or is something more needed? What does it mean for the gospel of the kingdom to be preached " 'in all the world as a witness to all the nations,' " or " 'to every nation, tribe, tongue, and people' "? (Matthew 24:14; Revelation 14:6).

Is it enough to go to every inhabited spot on earth and preach a single sermon? Is it possible to relay the full import of the gospel in such a way or over a satellite transmission?

Or did Jesus imply something more when He said that His gospel would " 'be preached in all the world as a witness to all the nations' "? (Matthew 24:14). What, exactly, has to happen before Jesus can return?

We'll continue our search for answers in the next chapter.

---

1. The entire introduction can be read at Marshall T. Savage's Internet website: http://www.millennial.org/intro/marshall.htm

CHAPTER 7

And Then the End

In *The Hitchhiker's Guide to the Galaxy,* Douglas Adams describes the end of the world. If you've focused your end-time reading on biblically oriented books, Adams's description is probably not like anything you've ever read. In his science-fiction spoof, the end of the world comes about suddenly, with only a few minutes' warning, at the hands of a construction crew building a new "hyperspatial express route" for travelers going from one planet to another. Earth is suddenly and unceremoniously blown to bits because it was in the way of a galaxywide construction project.

When earth inhabitants, who become aware of their impending demise a few minutes before the event, complain to the construction foreman, he seems incredulous. It's not like you didn't have a chance to protest long ago, he says. A notice about this construction project was posted fifty years ago on a planet just four light years away. If earth dwellers had only taken time to stop by, they'd have been able to file their protest before the construction crew arrived and perhaps had their planet spared or moved out of the way of the new express route.

Of course, no one really expects the end of the world to come about in that way, but Adams's tale does raise an interesting question.

At what point does a warning become a genuine warning? If it is posted in a place totally inaccessible to those who are to be warned, is it really a warning at all?

By the same token, when can a message be considered to have been delivered? Must it be received and understood, or must it only be sent?

In chapters 5 and 6 we looked at Jesus' prophecy that the gospel would be preached "in all the world, to every nation" before His Second Coming. We suggested that one possible reason why He has waited so long to return is that He has been waiting for a time when all the world would be connected together for instant communication.

But should we think of the *potential* for instant communication as *actual* communication?

I mean, if we Christians buy enough satellite time, we can certainly broadcast a sermon—maybe someone reading Jesus' Sermon on the Mount—to the whole world. We can make it available to every human who has access to a radio or television. We might want to add transmissions from a selection of shortwave radio stations, to reach people who don't listen to normal broadcast bands. Just to make sure we got maximum coverage, we could purchase advertisement banners on the most popular Internet portal sites like America Online, Yahoo, msn.com, and Alta Vista, with an intriguing come-on to get people to click and come to a site where the whole gospel message could be outlined in a few paragraphs. Or we could buy massive lists of e-mail addresses and send a sermon to every one of them.

I'm sure we could think up other publicity methods also, to assure that in just a few days' time our message could be made available to virtually every man, woman, and child on earth.

But is that what Jesus is waiting for?

If that's the impression I left you with in the last chapter, let me hasten to correct myself.

I don't believe that technology is the solution to the problem of getting the gospel to all the world. It certainly can play a role. But I don't think it will come about by Christians purchasing advertising time and preaching sermons on radio and television.

Sure, that type of thing helps. I spend most of my time these days developing scripts for Christian radio and television programs. At our Christian ministry we receive testimonial letters every week—people write in to thank us for helping them come to know Jesus as their Savior. So I know that our Christian broadcasts are having a positive impact in spreading the gospel to all the world.

But I don't believe that simply making the gospel available in this way will "finish the work" of spreading the good news of Jesus' kingdom " 'to every nation, kindred, tongue and people' " (Revelation 14:6, KJV). Let's face it, most of the people on earth will never listen to any Christian broadcast—or if they do happen to tune one in, they may skip on to another station or channel right away. If they aren't searching for spiritual insight, our preaching will fall on deaf ears.

No, I don't believe that preaching the gospel on the mass media will fulfill Jesus' prophecy that the gospel will go to all the world before the end comes. The media will help spread the word. And the ability to communicate instantly around the world is a cog on the wheel. It provides further opportunities for humanity to solve their own problems apart from God. In the overall great controversy scenario, mass communication provides one more test of Satan's claim that he can run the world better than God can. And in a moment we'll look at another role that mass communication can play in getting something more than just sermons about Jesus to the whole world.

What is the gospel?

But just for the sake of argument, let's take a moment to consider the question, What is the gospel? If we could buy thirty minutes of air time on every broadcast medium in the world, what would we do with those thirty minutes? What would we say? Who would be our spokesperson? Would it be possible to proclaim the gospel to all the world in thirty minutes? How about in an hour? Would four hours be long enough?

When I was in college, a little tract called something like "The Four Spiritual Questions" was popular. It was small enough that you could stick several in a shirt pocket or purse, and it was designed to help Christians make a "gospel presentation" to anyone they met.

The idea was that you could lead people through the four questions in the tract and talk to them for a few minutes about their soul's salvation and then ask whether they wanted to accept Jesus as their personal Savior. If a person said Yes, then he or she had heard and received the gospel and could now be considered a part of the kingdom of God.

Using that tract, you could present the gospel, close the deal for a soul's salvation, and be on your way to find another lost soul in fifteen minutes or less. The idea was quite popular in the era when microwave ovens were just coming into common usage.

At the time, the concept struck me as being somewhat inadequate, but I couldn't put my finger on just why.

Then, as I studied the gospel story in the Bible in greater depth, I came to understand what it was that bothered me about going from door to door making instant Christians.

The root of my questions lies in one simple, very familiar Bible verse: "And the Word became flesh and dwelt among us, and we beheld His glory, the glory as of the only begotten of the Father, full of grace and truth" (John 1:14).

The question boils down to this: If the good news—the gospel—could be adequately proclaimed in a radio or television message, or in a sermon preached in a synagogue or church, why did Jesus need to come to earth?

For thousands of years before Jesus' first coming, God had been proclaiming His message to the world through preachers and prophets, but somehow His message always ended up being misunderstood or misinterpreted or ignored.

People didn't fully understand the grace and truth of God until they saw it fleshed out in a human life. As the author of Hebrews puts it, "God, who at various times and in various ways spoke in time past to the fathers by the prophets, has in these last days spoken to us by His Son, whom He has appointed heir of all things, through whom also He made the worlds" (Hebrews 1:1, 2).

The prophets, in their preaching, speaking, and writing, fulfilled a vital role in letting people know about God and His will. But they were not perfect representatives of His grace and truth. Even pillars of faith like Job and Daniel didn't perfectly represent the depth of God's love for His children. Their lives served as worthy examples to emulate. But they were not perfect reflections of God's character.

So, in order to make the fullness of the gospel known, God sent His Son to earth to live and to die as a perfect example of what His grace and truth do in human flesh.

It's the difference between *telling* a man what to do and *showing* him how to do it. When Jesus said to Mary Magdalene, the woman caught in adultery, " 'Go and sin no more,' " He didn't leave her with a vague concept of dos and don'ts. He was right there in front of her, living His righteous life as an example to her. He stood in front of her, when she was naked and stripped of all her dignity, and looked right past her shame, down to her soul, and ministered the grace of God to her: " 'Neither do I condemn you,'" He said (John 8:11).

He gave her grace, and He lived the truth.

No wonder she became one of His most ardent followers. No wonder she was there at the foot of the cross. No wonder she was the one who stayed at the empty tomb until Jesus made an appearance.

She not only heard the gospel that day, she *saw* it. Jesus was and is the gospel. In His life He lived out the grace and truth of God.

Seeing the gospel

Historians tell us that no one ever sat down to write out the gospel—the good news about Jesus—until twenty-five or thirty years after He had ascended to heaven.

Jesus never assigned a scribe to sit down and take notes at His sermons, so that they could be preached again and again until the whole world had heard them.

Jesus didn't write a little red book of pearls of His wisdom and leave it behind for all of us to study.

What Jesus did leave behind was a group of men and women who had followed Him day after day, year after year, and had seen the grace and truth of God lived out in human flesh. He left behind people who had been through the mud, muck, and mire with Him and had watched the grace and truth of God operating in myriad difficult circumstances. Men and women who had been converted and changed by the love He bestowed upon them. Men like John, who once was known as a son of thunder because of his ready temper and willingness to call down fire from heaven but who became a loving, lovable person as he watched how Jesus lived.

When I was a young seminary student, my friend Les told me that it was possible to take a summer course in creation science in the form of fieldwork. What that meant was that the two of us could go out to Wyoming with Dr.

Harold Coffin and spend a month camping out and hiking around the mountains and get seminary credit for it.

I jumped at the chance. I've always been interested in creation science, and I love hiking and camping.

For five weeks that summer, Les and I traveled and camped and studied with Dr. Coffin. I no doubt learned a lot about geology, biology, and Creation during those weeks. But the one lesson that has really stuck with me was taught on a day our teacher may have considered wasted.

That was the day the lights on the travel trailer Dr. Coffin towed with him started acting up.

If you've ever worked on lights on a travel trailer, you know how frustrating it can be. There's something confoundedly contrary about those things. We stopped beside the road to work on them. When the brake lights would work, the blinkers would quit working, and when we got that fixed, the running lights would malfunction.

I worked with Les and Dr. Coffin for two hours but finally gave up in frustration and suggested we go to a garage and let an electrician fix the problem. But Dr. Coffin wanted to keep trying it on his own. Les stuck with him, but I just sat down and started reading our textbook.

They worked on those lights for two more hours.

And then two more hours.

And then two more hours. And finally, after eight hours of trying this, that, and the other thing, they got it right.

And all that time Dr. Coffin never spoke a word in frustration, never kicked a tire, never slammed his fist into the siding, never sat down and pounded on the ground. He just kept patiently working, trying one thing and then another until he finally had solved his problem.

I have to confess: I still don't have the patience to work quietly for that long on a frustrating problem. I fear that if I'd continued working with Dr. Coffin, his trailer would still have fist-shaped dents today.

But Dr. Coffin's quiet lesson in patience and perseverance has stayed with me. I continue to carry it around in my mind as an example to emulate.

That type of living makes an impression that goes on and on. Patience and grace lived out, particularly in times of difficulty and trial, get people's attention.

And that's why Jesus came to earth to dwell among us.

And that's why, when the disciples and others finally sat down to write out the gospel, they didn't give us transcripts of Jesus' sermons. They told us stories about Him.

The disciples had watched in open-mouthed awe as Jesus moved from place to place, always bestowing grace on those He encountered, whether they deserved it or not. They had listened, even as He spoke roughly to those who thought they had righteousness all figured out and sewed to their shirt sleeves. They had seen that in each instance His concern was to shake people loose from their apathy and to turn their eyes toward heaven and the true righteousness and grace of God.

And then they had watched His response when all the world turned against Him. Peter, testifying years later about Jesus' response under unimaginably trying circumstances, wrote these memorable words: "who, when He was reviled, did not revile in return; when He suffered, He did not threaten, but committed Himself to Him who judges righteously" (1 Peter 2:23).

Paul, emulating his Master, could say of himself and his companions: "And we labor, working with our own hands. Being reviled, we bless; being persecuted, we endure" (1 Corinthians 4:12).

Paul, Peter, and the other apostles had learned that the way to spread the gospel is to live it. They could not be perfect examples of holiness as Jesus was, but they could tell how He had transformed their lives and how He was continuing to do so. They could endure trials with patience, returning love for hatred.

And they could talk about Jesus.

That's what Jesus intended to happen when He ascended. That's why He left behind disciples, not transcripts.

Because the gospel needs to be fleshed out.

More than words can tell

As far as we know, the apostle Paul never saw Jesus while He was on earth—at least Paul never tells us that he did. But Paul did encounter Jesus on the road to Damascus. And that brief, direct encounter changed his life. Immediately he wanted to know more about Jesus. He wanted to live as Jesus lived. And when he set out to evangelize the world, he realized that merely telling people about Jesus would not be enough. He had to show people how to live the gospel.

In Thessalonica he and Silas shared the gospel, and a Christian church soon formed in the city. Paul and his companions had to leave abruptly due to opposition, but later he took time to write two letters back to the Thessalonians. In his first letter he reminded them that he did much more than just preach to them when he was there. He not only spoke but lived the gospel: "For our gospel did not come to you in word only, but also in power, and in the Holy Spirit and in much assurance, as you know what kind of men we were among you for your sake" (1 Thessalonians 1:5).

"You know what kind of men we were," he says. They were Christian men, living as Jesus lived, lives worthy of emulation. They didn't just tell the people about Jesus, they lived as Jesus would among them. When things turned against them, they didn't strike back but simply went on to a new area to proclaim and live the gospel.

Because he had learned to live as Jesus did, Paul could write to the Corinthians, "Imitate me, just as I also imitate Christ" (1 Corinthians 11:1).

And what were the results of this method of spreading the good news about Jesus?

"And you became followers of us and of the Lord, having received the word in much affliction, with joy of the Holy Spirit, so that you became examples to all in Macedonia and Achaia who believe" (1 Thessalonians 1:6, 7).

The gospel, lived out, becomes contagious and spreads like fire in August hayfields.

Preaching can be ignored or argued with. But when people start living as Jesus did, the world takes notice. "Mother Teresa" is a name known around the world, not for what she said but for how she lived.

But does that mean that in order for the gospel to truly be spread to every nation, kindred, tongue, etc., real, live, in-the-flesh-perfect Christians need to go and live in every village and town on earth?

Would that really accomplish spreading the gospel? In most cities, and even in small villages, a new person in town only mingles with a few people. Even planting a church in every community would not assure that the gospel was presented to all the world. Churches by nature tend to reach only a certain group of people in their community, leaving others unevangelized.

So, how can the gospel go to all the world?

An end-time scenario

Let's pull together the ideas from previous chapters and mix them up with what we've talked about in this chapter and see if we find answers to any of the questions we've been asking.

The thing that most caught people's attention about

JESUS FOR A NEW MILLENNIUM

Jesus was the way He responded to trial. He didn't strike back. He continued to live out the grace and truth of God. Even on the cross He could pray " 'Father, forgive them, for they know not what they do.' " That was the gospel in a nutshell. The grace of God shining through in the most horrific of circumstances.

We noticed earlier that Jesus pointed out that other things would happen after the wars, famines, earthquakes, and other disasters that constituted "the beginning of sorrows."

Jesus calls these things "the beginning of sorrows" in Matthew 24:8. Let's read all of the next several verses, up to verse 14, where He speaks of the gospel going to all the world and notice what happens between the time of "the beginning of sorrows" and the end:

> Then they will deliver you up to tribulation and kill you, and you will be hated by all nations for My name's sake. And then many will be offended, will betray one another, and will hate one another. Then many false prophets will rise up and deceive many. And because lawlessness will abound, the love of many will grow cold. But he who endures to the end shall be saved. And this gospel of the kingdom will be preached in all the world as a witness to all the nations, and then the end will come (Matthew 24:9-14).

Notice this: After the physical signs of the end come the spiritual signs of the end: Persecution, hatred, tribulation fall upon the followers of Jesus. Hatred replaces love among many, and Christians betray one another to their enemies. Many who have not been settled firmly into the grace and truth of Jesus will go astray under the leadership of false prophets. Lawlessness will be the rule of the day, and under these trying, anarchical circumstances, many Christians will lose the experience of love they once had. Probably they will begin to strike back at those who persecute them. When reviled, they will not emulate their Master but will revile back.

This time of trial, lawlessness, betrayal, and deception is a testing time. It is the heat of the summer that ripens the harvest, separating the wheat from the tares.

But it is something more, as well.

In the midst of this there will be some who endure to the end.

There will be some who, despite the persecution, despite the "time of trouble, such as never was since there was a nation, even to that time" (Daniel 12:1), will "endure to the end." Some whose love will not grow cold even in hardship. Some who will continue to live like Jesus. Some who, even when they are tortured or put to death for their faith, will look around them and pray for the forgiveness of their persecutors.

Immediately after Jesus spoke of those brave, faithful, enduring souls, He predicted that the gospel would go to all the world, and then the end would come.

Now, persecution, trials, and martyrdom have happened all through the centuries. Thousands of devout believers perished in the persecutions of the pagan Caesars in the first centuries of the church's existence. Some were torn apart by lions, while others were used as living torches at Nero's palace. There has hardly been a time in the history of Christianity when some were not dying for their faith.

During the Roman persecution of the first few centuries, the church father Tertullian penned his famous line about "the blood of the martyrs is the seed of the gospel." And truly those who went to their deaths strong in their faith did inspire many others to give their lives to Christ.

But never, in all those centuries, did the martyrdom and persecution lead to the gospel going to all the world.

Much of the world had not even been discovered by Christians yet.

And the spread of news was limited.

But Jesus predicted that just before the gospel went to all the world, and after the other signs had been fulfilled, another time of terrible trouble for Christians would come. Christians will be persecuted and put to the test just as Jesus was.

Now, imagine, with our communication potential today, what will happen when full-scale persecution once again breaks out against Christians.

Word will spread worldwide in no time. Every Christian on every continent will be faced with the same sort of decision: How will I respond when they come for me? Will I hunker in a bunker with an AK-47 and dare them to try to take me? Or will I be like Jesus who told Peter to put his sword away and surrendered when the soldiers came for Him in Gethsemane?

How will I respond when they mock me, spit on me, beat me within an inch of my life? Will I curse them, or will I pray for them? If they drive nails through my hands and feet and hang me up naked and stand around insulting me and my God, will I still be able to pray for their forgiveness?

Not everyone who claims the name of Christian today will be able to do that. That's why so many will fall away. Their love will suddenly turn to ice in the face of such prospects. It will be every man for himself, every woman for herself. Even the children will turn against their parents.

But in the midst of this time of trial and apostasy, there will be a few, the elect, Jesus called them, who will "endure to the end" and be saved.

And that word will go worldwide instantly as well.

Imagine it.

Virtually the whole world—including many former Christians—will be united against these few, true Christians. They'll be put to trial. And the news will go worldwide. People everywhere will be aware.

These few, these elect, wherever they are, will be tested to the uttermost with all the world watching.

They will have the chance to act like Jesus on a truly global stage like no other that has ever existed.

And they'll live out the gospel as a testimony to every man, woman, and child on the planet.

Through them, through their lives, and in many cases through their deaths as martyrs, the gospel will be preached to all the world. Thousands, perhaps millions, watching them may be converted as the truth about God's love, grace, and forgivness is fleshed out in the most trying circumstances.

It's a frightening prospect but also a glorious one.

But some questions still remain.

How and why will the world come to a time when Christians are put on trial on a world stage? And is there a timetable that reveals when this will happen?

We noticed in chapter 3 that the prophet Daniel set out the timetable that revealed when Jesus would come the first time. The good news is that his book, along with the New Testament book of Revelation, give additional clues that help us to understand the closing events of the end time of earth's history.

We'll take a look at these prophecies in chapter 8.

The Time of the End

As I write these words, the world is about as peaceful as it ever gets. The NATO bombing campaign in Serbia has yielded at least some of its intended results—Serbian troops have withdrawn from Kosovo. For the time being.

India and Pakistan are keeping their war to the level of a backroom squabble to keep from attracting too much attention. The two Koreas are trading threats but only occasional blows. The Turks are about to execute one of their chief Kurdish enemies, which will either strike fear in the hearts of other potential rebels or provoke his friends to greater valor. There are some long-standing civil wars going on in Africa, and there is basically no government that can keep peace yet in Somalia. The most recent war count I've been able to locate comes from the end of 1996, when the United Nations Commission on Human Rights reported that there were thirty-four active wars going on in the world and twenty near-wars. Some of these have, no doubt, been resolved by now, but others have flared up to take their place.

Still, overall things are about as peaceful as they can ever get on a planet peopled by human beings. The new Israeli prime minister recently met and shook hands with Yasser Arafat, promising new efforts toward peace.

In recent years there has been a strong push for greater

tolerance, but persecution based on religion does still happen. A Roman Catholic priest from a country controlled by a non-Christian government reported that he was arrested and held in jail for four months in 1996 chiefly because he was a Christian. While in jail he was tortured; given electric shocks to the head, armpits, and genitals; and burned with cigarettes. After his release he had to go into hiding and finally took refuge in an embassy in order to get out of the country.

Similar incidents of persecution between religions are reported from other countries including Iran, China, and Burma. In Northern Ireland, people calling themselves Christians regularly blow each other to bits with bombs.

But in large areas of the world, people of various backgrounds and beliefs live side by side in tolerance, if not in harmony. The overall trend of the world is toward what the United Nations refers to as "greater democratization." In other words, the world is moving in the direction of greater equality of human rights.

This hardly seems like the type of conditions Jesus predicted would prevail just before His return. Remember what He said in Matthew 24:9: " 'Then they will deliver you up to tribulation and kill you, and you will be hated by all nations for My name's sake.' "

If our world is moving toward greater tolerance, why did Jesus predict the opposite for the time just before His return? And if we take His prophecy to heart, does that mean we shouldn't expect Him back anytime soon?

The prophetic background

Jesus was familiar with the writings of the Old Testament prophets. He often quoted them or cited their stories. And, of course, He paid especially close attention to the prophecies of Daniel, because it was the last few verses of Daniel 9 that pointed to the exact year when He would be baptized in the Jordan and begin His ministry.

It was Daniel who recorded an angel's prediction that there would be a "a time of trouble, such as never was since there was a nation, even to that time" (Daniel 12:1) at the end of earth's history.

Going beyond those sketchy details, Daniel made some rather startling predictions. In chapters 2, 7, and 8, he laid out a prophetic scenario that continues to be fulfilled today. Writing more than five hundred years before the birth of Jesus, during the time of the Babylonian and Medo-Persian Empires, Daniel opened the pages of the future, predicting Alexander the Great's rampages on the world stage and the later rise and fall of the Roman Empire.

Looking farther into the future, he predicted the rise of a particularly nefarious religious power that would cause God's true servants to be persecuted right down to the end of time.

Daniel painted these scenes with broad-brushed strokes but hid a few startling clues on the canvas to help us identify the events, powers, and times involved.

Then Jesus, after His ascension, spoke to His beloved disciple John in the visions that are recorded in the book of Revelation.

Putting together the prophecies of Daniel with those of Revelation yields a composite picture of conditions in the world just before Jesus returns. Better yet, the picture reveals the powers and events that will bring the world to those conditions. I'm going to give just a quick overview of these predictions here. If you'd like to study the underlying prophetic scenario in greater detail, I highly recommend the series of Bible study guides produced by the Voice of Prophecy. These Discover Bible Guides are available free of charge by writing to Discover Bible School, Voice of Prophecy, Box 53055, Los Angeles, CA 99053. Or better yet, you can enroll for free in the Bible School on the Internet by visiting the Voice of Prophecy website at http://www.vop.com. After you've done the basic Discover course, you'll probably want to continue on with the advanced courses covering the books of Daniel and Revelation.

But for now, here's a basic overview of what Daniel and Revelation predict will happen before Jesus returns.

Beginning with events that were happening in his own day, Daniel depicted the rise and fall of empires including the Babylonian, Medo-Persian, Greek, and Roman. In Daniel 7 and 8 the various empires are each pictured as beasts with characteristics that symbolize the actions of the empires. Following the dissolution of the Roman Empire (the only one of the four that he didn't see falling victim to another empire), Daniel predicted a time of disunity with no one empire controlling the world in the way that the earlier powers had.

But Daniel did see a blasphemous religious power rising out of Rome in the empire's wake. In vision Daniel saw it represented as a "little horn" with its roots in Rome. Daniel's prophecy predicted that this little horn would stand in opposition to God and His people and would have power to persecute them for a time period referred to in Daniel 7:25 as "a time and times and half a time." This enigmatic time period comes up over and over in Daniel and Revelation (see Daniel 12:7; Revelation 12:14). It's also spoken of as forty-two months (Revelation 11:2; 13:5) and as 1,260 days (Revelation 11:3; 12:6). Using the "day for a year" principle of prophetic interpretation, this time period has historically been interpreted by Protestant Christians as referring to 1,260 years.

They say hindsight is always 20/20, so Bible students in the 1800s began to look back over the period of history immediately following the dissolution of the Roman Empire in about A.D. 476, searching for clues as to whether this 1,260 years of persecution had already ended or whether it was still going on. As they studied the history, they came to the startling conclusion that this prophecy had already come to an end, not long before their day. They were even able to fix the starting and ending years as A.D. 538 and A.D. 1798!

I won't take time here to go into the details of how this was worked out (once again, if you're interested, see my note above about the Discover Bible School). Suffice it to say that much of the time from 538 to 1798 is referred to as the Dark Ages, when there was very little spiritual enlightenment available. Christianity had, for the most part, fallen under the totalitarian control of a Roman-based religious system that kept the general populace ignorant of the true message of the gospel. Thousands of people who tried to stand up for Bible truth during those years were persecuted, and many died for their faith at the hands of this apostate religious power. This was what Daniel's visions had predicted would happen.

The time of the end

Daniel's prophecies pointed to the "time of the end" as a time *after* this 1,260-year period had run its course (see Daniel 12:1-9). And Daniel was told that in this "time of the end" people would be running "to and fro" and knowledge would be on the increase.

These prophecies have certainly been fulfilled, for since the end of that prophetic period in 1798 things have changed drastically in our world—mostly as a result of the fantastic explosion of knowledge. We've been through the industrial age, the steam age, the air age, the jet age, the space age, and now we're in what's known as the information age. Because the world is so closely tied together by the Internet and other media today, knowledge is growing and spreading faster than ever. A study released in July of 1999 revealed that in 1998 and the first half of 1999 the number of individual web pages on the Internet had nearly tripled. There are now more than 800 million web pages accessible to viewers the world over.

As I pointed out in chapter 5, Daniel's prophecies also pointed to another special year in our era. The longest time prophecy in the Bible is found in Daniel 8, and it pointed to the year 1844 as an important year in Jesus' plans and preparations for His return to earth.

These time prophecies were not as specific as the prophecy in Daniel 9, which pointed to the exact year that Jesus would begin His ministry on earth, but they put us in the ballpark, so to speak.

Because all these time prophecies have run their course, we can know that our current era is what the Bible calls "the time of the end."

Daniel's prophecies focused mainly on events that are already past now, but in Revelation Jesus picked up where Daniel left off and gave John a more detailed look at the forces that will come into play just before the Second Coming—forces that will bring about the trying conditions that will separate the gold from the dross among professing Christians.

One of the most detailed prophecies about this future time is found in Revelation 13. This chapter starts with a picture of a beast that represents the same persecuting power that Daniel described in chapter 7—the little-horn power with roots in Rome that persecuted true Christians for 1,260 years (Revelation 13:5 refers to this time as forty-two months—42 months x 30 days/month = 1,260 days).

Revelation 13:5-7 parallels Daniel's prophecy about the persecuting power that would come after Rome. But this prophecy expired in 1798. Since then we've been living in what the Bible refers to as "the end of time."

Do you suppose God would leave us to go through this time without any prophecies to help us know what to expect?

Of course not.

Revelation 13 doesn't end with verse 7. It goes on and describes another persecuting power that would come upon the earth as the successor to the beast described in verses 5-7. Take a look at the description in verse 11: "Then I saw another beast coming up out of the earth, and he had two horns like a lamb and spoke like a dragon."

This new beast arrives on the scene just at the time when the other beast's 1,260 years have expired. And notice—he seems like a gentle, harmless lamb at first.

But then he opens his mouth. And the words that come out are dragon words.

In Revelation the dragon is a symbol of Satan (Revelation 12:9). And it soon becomes apparent that this lamblike beast's agenda is the same as that of the persecuting power before him, and that is Satan's agenda. Revelation 13:4 says that the first beast got his authority from the dragon and caused people to worship the dragon. And verse 12 says that the new beast "exercises all the authority of the first beast in his presence, and causes the earth and those who dwell in it to worship the first beast."

The line of authority runs straight and true. The second beast draws his authority from the first beast. The first beast draws his authority straight from Satan.

Is it any wonder then that in the last days when the power represented by this second beast takes control of the earth anyone who remains true to God will come under fierce persecution? Revelation 13 tells the story in terms reminiscent of the familiar story in Daniel 3, where Daniel's three friends were commanded to bow down and worship an image that stood for the power of Babylon's King Nebuchadnezzar.

The second beast creates an image in honor of the first beast then brings the image to life. And next, of course, he orders everyone on earth to bow down to it: "He was granted power to give breath to the image of the beast, that the image of the beast should both speak and cause as many as would not worship the image of the beast to be killed" (Revelation 13:15).

In Daniel's story the three faithful young men who refused to bow down soon faced the ultimate test of their faith in God. When they refused to turn from their God to worship the image, they were thrown into a superheated fiery furnace.

In the same way, those who refuse to bow down to the "image of the beast" in the end times will face a superheated trial of their faith.

It comes down to a life and death decision for every person on earth. There are only two options: Worship the image that represents Satan's power or be prepared to die.

The next verses tell of the time when all who want life to go on as usual—buying and selling the things needed for a normal life—will have to receive the "mark of the beast."

The beast represents all that stands in opposition to God. It represents humanity apart from the grace of God, for the number of the beast is the number of man apart from God. God's number, the number of perfection, is seven, and God is a Trinity, so the number of God is 777. The number of the beast, the number of man, is just one shy on every count: 666. "This calls for wisdom. If anyone has insight, let him calculate the number of the beast, for it is man's number. His number is 666" (Revelation 13:18, NIV).

The issue of the *cross*

The issues at stake at the end of time, when everyone has to decide whether to entrust themselves into God's care or to do things their own way, are the same issues that Jesus faced when He was on earth. He faced them when He met the devil in the wilderness after fasting for more than a month. He faced them daily when He encountered obstacles, irritations, and obstinate people. He faced them in all the strength of their raw, flesh-rending force on the cross.

The question to be answered in each situation was the same: Could Satan push the right buttons to get Jesus to respond in an ungodly, ungracious way? Could he push Jesus hard enough that He would push back? Could he make the pain and humiliation so overpowering that Jesus would lose sight of His mission, lose faith in His Father, lose contact with the Holy Spirit, and let His fleshly reactions take over? Could he get through to the human, knee-jerk reflex that spits back when spat upon, that calls down curses in response to mocking, reviling, and torture?

If he could do that, the battle for control of the universe would be over. The character of God would be revealed to be no better than Satan's. The God of the Hebrews would be shown to be no different from the Greek and Roman gods who fought out their petty squabbles on Mount Olympus, trading imprecation for insult and thunderbolt for tempest.

All the universe watched the center cross on Calvary to see how God would behave under stress and persecution.

Thank God that Jesus managed to live out the gospel—the good news about God—for all to see.

He lived it out in what He said and what He did.

Peter, who was there watching, aghast and humbled, testified of Jesus who "when He was reviled, did not revile in return; when He suffered, He did not threaten, but committed Himself to Him who judges righteously" (1 Peter 2:23).

John was there and witnessed that even in the severest of suffering, and on the point of death, Jesus was more concerned for the needs of others than for Himself. He arranged for John to care for His mother in His absence.

Luke tells us that instead of striking back at those who were driving nails through His flesh, Jesus prayed for them—prayed for their forgiveness. " 'Father, forgive them, for they do not know what they do,' " He prayed (Luke 23:34).

Despite His suffering, Jesus maintained His interest

in the salvation of souls. When a common thief expressed faith in Him, Jesus accepted it and accepted him into His kingdom.

When it came down to a life-and-death decision for Jesus, He chose death rather than surrender.

But even more important was the *way* He died.

He didn't go down to death kicking and screaming and reminding His tormentors that He'd be back someday and then they'd see who had the last laugh—and the last scream!

He didn't drink the bitter cup willingly—He pled with His Father to remove it if possible. But when it could not be taken away, He accepted it without complaint and without trying to get even with those who mixed all the accumulated gall of millennia of evil into a cup of searing pain and thrust it in His face.

The gospel in the flesh

That's how Jesus lived out the gospel for all to see.

But that happened in a remote corner of the Roman Empire, and though word spread quickly in the Roman world, centuries would pass before word of what the Son of God had done at Calvary spread much beyond the empire's borders.

And all too often, when the Christian message has been carried around the world, it has arrived at its destination in diluted form. Only certain aspects of the message seem to have gotten through in Northern Ireland, for example.

I don't mean to pick on the Irish. My roots go back to the Emerald Isle. But somehow the people of that fair land who blow up marketplaces in the name of their Christian faith have gotten a diluted picture of Jesus. They've missed the whole point of the Cross. They worship a Jesus who strikes back at those who inflict pain, not the real Jesus who prayed "Father, forgive them!"

Somehow the gospel message has been polluted in Serbia as well, and Christian soldiers consider it honorable to rape, maim, and kill Moslems and Christians of a different heritage.

One of the most poignant stories to come out of the recent conflict in Kosovo was buried at the end of a *New York Times* article about the withdrawal of Yugoslav troops from Kosovo. The story no doubt typifies what happened in villages throughout the ruined province, but what caught my eye was the name of the place where it was reported from. Here's the last paragraph of that article:

> In the village of Grace, north of Pristina, Albanians took whatever they could from houses after driving out the Serbs who lived there. "Everything they did to us, we're getting back now," said Gazmehd Kosumi, 25, who returned with his family two days ago to find their two homes nearby destroyed. "They burned everything. They took everything."[1]

That such a thing should happen in a place called Grace!

The actions of both the Serbian Christians and the Albanian Moslems are the antithesis of grace. The antithesis of what Jesus demonstrated on the cross. But they are all too natural. All too human. All too much like me.

I can't stand back and point a judgmental finger at those who have made intimidation and retaliation a way of life for generations, for I have not walked in their shoes. I do not know how I would respond in their circumstances.

But because of what Jesus did, I know how a Christian should respond.

Because of what happened on the cross of Christ, I know how those who have learned to flesh out the gospel will respond to extreme circumstances today and in the persecution that will come in the last days.

What a challenge! What a level of grace to strive for. It's not something I can achieve on my own. Only the grace of God can empower weak, human bodies to flesh out the gospel in the time when " 'because lawlessness will abound the love of many will grow cold' " (Matthew 24:12).

As we've built our character profile of Jesus, I think you've noticed that He is trustworthy. We can trust Him to see us through whatever comes our way. And He is strong—having been through suffering and trial Himself, He can strengthen us and understand our needs. And He is gracious. Gracious enough to forgive us, cleanse us, and make us over in His image so that we can live, and if need be, die as He did.

Grace in the last days

Imagine it.

In our age of technology, when all the world is so closely connected together, when what happens in Manhattan or in Timbuktu can instantly be beamed to the whole world, imagine a scenario where Christians are put to the test.

Imagine a world united behind the authority of the second beast of Revelation 13, taking orders from Satan's command center via the first beast.

It's a time when many Christians have already faded into the woodwork—abandoning their faith when it came down to a question of enduring persecution and pain for their beliefs. It's a time when " 'many [professed Christians] will fall away and will deliver up one another and hate one another' " (Matthew 24:10, NASB).

Imagine now, the few remaining ones who have kept their eyes focused on Jesus, who have not only remembered how He reacted when His friends betrayed and abandoned Him but have learned to let His spirit provoke the same reactions in themselves.

Imagine when all the world's hatred is focused against these true believers. Imagine a show trial where they are put on display as a warning to all the world. Or perhaps simultaneous trials in many different parts of the world. They are tortured for their faith, perhaps even crucified as their Lord was.

How do they respond?

What does the world see?

It sees the gospel lived out in the flesh.

It sees the gospel of Jesus Christ portrayed in stark contrast to every other method of salvation in the world.

Atheists who have chosen not to believe in God because of the hateful version of Christianity they have encountered are suddenly confronted with images of people whose lives have obviously been supernaturally empowered by love and grace. Moslems who have been taught that Jesus is a weak Savior because He was crucified suddenly see how much courage and strength it takes to live as a true Christian. Hindus and Buddhists who have been taught that their only hope of salvation lies in living out thousands of lives in which there is no forgiveness but only karma spinning its endless rounds of justice and retribution are confronted with people who are praying for grace and forgiveness even for those who are doing evil to them.

The world's attention is captured in a way no missionary, no sermon, ever could.

And the gospel is, under those circumstances, instantly presented in all its fleshed-out fullness to all the world.

The story is told and retold in cities, slums, villages, and penthouses. Not by paid missionaries but by people who have witnessed the gospel with their own eyes—shocked by its fleshed out grace and love.

And every man, woman, and child on earth is given the chance to consider the message that Jesus lived out on the cross.

Imagine it. In a matter of hours, or days at the most, the whole world could hear the gospel, not as mere words, but as the fleshed-out, four-dimensional reality that only a human life, lived in time and space, can portray.

Words can't express the excitement I feel when I consider this picture.

It's a frightening prospect in a way, isn't it? To think that I as a Christian may be called upon to live out the gospel in such circumstances. And yet what a privilege—to stand on the world stage as a representative of the King of the universe!

I've often pondered texts like Philippians 1:29, which say that it has been given to us (as a gift) not only to believe in Jesus "but also to suffer for His sake"; Philippians 3:10 where Paul prays for the privilege of knowing "the fellowship of His sufferings" and being "conformed to His death"; and 1 Peter 4:19, which speaks of "those who suffer according to the will of God."

I've been tempted at times to think perhaps that the two greatest apostles were infected with a touch of masochism—why else would they *want* to know the fellowship of Jesus' sufferings? I mean, I hate to go to the dentist. Surely no normal person looks forward to having pain inflicted.

But what if my response to suffering could serve as a testimony to the whole world? What if I should be given the privilege of living out Jesus' gospel attitude toward those who tortured Him? What if my life could witness the good news of God's offer of forgiveness to all of the six or seven billion people on earth? Forgiveness offered even to the most demon-driven, depraved torturers ever to walk the face of the earth.

If people could see that, wouldn't at least some respond and ask God to come into their hearts and make them over in the image of Jesus too? Perhaps some who had never had a chance to *hear* the gospel *preached.*

Isn't that what Jesus is waiting for?

For the maximum number of people possible to see the gospel lived out and to have the chance to choose Him as their Savior for all eternity.

It's a scary picture but also a glorious one.

" 'Then they will deliver you up to tribulation and kill you, and you will be hated by all nations for My name's sake. And then many will be offended, will betray one another, and will hate one another. Then many false prophets will rise up and deceive many. And because lawlessness will abound, the love of many will grow cold. But he who endures to the end shall be saved. And this gospel of the kingdom will be preached in all the world as a witness to all the nations, *and then the end will come*' " (Matthew 24:9-14).

---

[1] Steven Lee Myers, "Yugoslav Troops Clear Out of Kosovo," printed in Los Angeles *Daily News* June 21, 1999. Byline cites *The New York Times*.

CHAPTER 9

I Want to Be Ready

Do you think that Jesus will come in the year 2000? Or perhaps 2001? Will He come early in this new millennium? Or do we still have a long time to wait for the things we've seen prophesied to come about?

Certainly things can change fast in our world. The sudden collapse of communism at the end of the last decade caught almost everyone by surprise, as did the sudden alliance of nations against Iraq, and NATO's continuing unity in attacking Slobodan Milosevic's Serbian troops in Kosovo.

It seems that all the pieces are in place for sudden unification of the world for or against almost any group that evokes the popular leadership's ire. And the worldwide stage is in place, just waiting for the final conflict between the forces of good and evil to be played out while all the world watches.

While the year 2000 isn't really Jesus' two-thousandth birthday, it does fall at a time when the things that Jesus said would occur at the end can rapidly fall into place. And it does come after the ending date of the longest time prophecy (see chapter 5).

So, it could happen. The final events leading up to the climax of history could all tumble together with lightning speed, catching everyone by surprise. Who knows what sort of crisis might bring it on? Some of my friends believe the stimulus will be the approach of a killer asteroid. I played out that scenario, along with a major push by demonic spirits, in my book *The Orion Conspiracy*. But events of recent years have shown that it might not take anything as drastic as that to unite world powers in a push for unity at the expense of conscience.

We are living in a time like no other in history. A time that really and truly fulfills the expectations set up by Jesus in His discourse on the last days. I have in my library a collection of old books about prophecy, and it's amusing to go through them and see how authors seventy or a hundred years ago looked for evidences that their day met these criteria. One shows a speeding steam engine as an evidence of men running to and fro and linking the whole world together at high speed. A more recent one shows a propeller-driven airliner as evidence of quick worldwide communication.

But those things were all steps toward our present day, when instant communication truly is available. No doubt, if time continues, the worldwide linkage will grow even closer and faster. But it hardly seems necessary.

So it seems that the end could come quickly.

Is there anything further that Jesus might still be waiting for?

Hastening the day

Consider this counsel from Peter, the man who was converted by watching Jesus deal with His time of trial:

But the day of the Lord will come as a thief in the night, in which the heavens will pass away with a great noise, and the elements will melt with fervent heat; both the earth and the works that are in it will be burned up. Therefore, since all these things will be dissolved, what manner of persons ought you to be in holy conduct and godliness, looking for and hastening the coming of the day of God, because of which the heavens will be dissolved, being on fire, and the elements will melt with fervent heat? (2 Peter 2:10-12).

Notice that when Peter speaks of the end of the world, he doesn't just focus on the events that will happen. He turns the focus back to us. Gazing forward to events yet to happen, he quickly turns his head, looks back over his shoulder, and speaks to the congregation of Christians who are expecting these things: Since we know all of this is coming, what should we be doing to prepare for it? Indeed, what should we be doing to hasten—to hurry up—the coming of that day?

For centuries scholars have debated what Peter meant here. After all, if God already knows the day and hour of Christ's return, why should we even consider that anything we might do could hasten the day?

I can't say that I have an adequate answer to that question, but it seems to me that Peter recognized that there was a human element involved in putting all the pieces together for the final day.

We've noticed that all the pieces seem to be in place for the final trial and persecution of Christians to begin. But there is one human element we can't be sure about until the time of trial comes.

Is there a group of Christians in place, ready to face the time of fiery trial? Are there people who are settled soundly enough into the grace and truth of Jesus that they will not be deceived by the false prophets? Is there a group whose love will not grow cold even in the most deprived, depraved, and degrading of circumstances? Are there people whose love is strong enough that they won't turn against a brother or sister to save their own skin?

In short, is there a group who knows Jesus well enough, and walks with Him closely enough, that it will bear its time of trial in the same way that He did?

Am I a part of that group?

Am I one of those who could endure all of that to the very bitter end? Would the way I live stand as a testimony for Jesus on that worldwide stage?

It's impossible to know how we will handle a crisis before it comes.

But we can look for clues in the way we handle the little crises that come our way each day.

Am I, by the grace of God, developing the patience of Job and Jesus? Are you?

When someone does me wrong, do I find it natural to forgive?

If I had to surrender everything I own, and even my life, to spare the life of a brother, would I do it?

These are hard questions. Ones I don't feel comfortable answering. I know that if I face these tests, it will be only by the grace of God and my personal, abiding faith in Jesus, built on a rock-solid relationship with Jesus, that I will be able to endure to the end.

How about you? Do you feel confident that you could pass these tests?

If not (or even if you do), take a moment to consider with me some of the gifts that God has given us that are designed to help us be ready for the time of trial. He doesn't ask us to face a time of trial without preparation. In the Bible He has given us a training course.

Preparing for the day

In this section I want to briefly review some of the central, core teachings of Jesus. Teachings that He gave us that are designed to help us remain close to Him and develop the kind of faith and relationship that will enable us to be like Him and to respond to trial in the same way He did.

Time spent with Jesus. That's why He came to earth. That's why He chose disciples to follow Him wherever He went. He knew that the key to turning these men of various personalities and propensities into people who would live out the gospel in the world was for them to spend time with Him.

If you're not having regular devotional time in which you sit at the feet of Jesus and learn of Him, get started right now. When the time of trial comes, it will be difficult, if not impossible, to build the kind of trusting relationship you need.

But in addition to that daily devotional time, remember that Jesus, as the Creator of the world, gave us a special time each week when we could put aside the things of the world and focus on developing our relationship with Him. It's called the Sabbath. Unfortunately much of the Christian world has lost sight of this wonderful gift. Christian teachers have argued that Jesus did away with the Sabbath, but He did no such thing.

Why would He want to eliminate this special day for fellowship with the people He was seeking to mold into His image? No, Jesus didn't do away with the Sabbath. When the Pharisees challenged the way He kept the Sabbath, He didn't say "the Sabbath is done away with." No way. He simply said " 'The Sabbath was made for man, and not man for the Sabbath' " (Mark 2:27).

The Pharisees had been treating the Sabbath as a negative—a day that God had taken away from humankind. Jesus turned the tables on them and reminded us that God didn't take the Sabbath away but gave it to us as a day for special fellowship with Him.

Jesus didn't do away with the Sabbath. But instead of telling us what *not* to do on the Sabbath, which was what the Pharisees liked to emphasize, He told us what we *ought* to do on the Sabbath: " 'Therefore it is lawful to do good on the Sabbath,' " He said (Matthew 12:12).

All that Jesus did away with was the negative aspects of Sabbath observance. He turned it from a negative "don't" day to a positive "do" day. We can act like Jesus on the Sabbath, reaching out and touching and healing our world. We can walk with Jesus on that day, learning to be like Him.

For many people, the issue of Sabbath observance has been reduced to a dispute about which day is proper to keep. And it is important to learn to accept God's instructions on issues like this and to worship on the day He set aside rather than a day I may choose. But the "which day" question can become a sidetrack that leads us away from the real purpose of the day—learning to spend time consistently and regularly with God. Learning to grow our faith through time spent with Him. Learning to put aside our attempts to save ourselves.

Of all the keys to being ready for the end time, nothing is more important than spending time with Jesus.

But there are other aspects of biblical teaching that Jesus put in place in order to help us as well. Things that can help to mold our character and develop our faith to enable us to live as He lived and to endure trial as He did.

Good stewardship is one of these. In several of His parables Jesus spoke of the "wise steward" or the "faithful servant" who took proper care of his master's possessions. In Matthew 24 He describes the "faithful and wise servant" whom the master leaves in charge of his servants and who tends to the needs of the household staff properly. In contrast, He describes a wicked servant who takes his master's goods for himself and eats and drinks with the drunkards.

This parable is directly linked to Jesus' teaching about the Second Coming, so we ought to look carefully at what it teaches.

Stewardship has always been an important part of a relationship to God. In fact, in the Old Testament, worship consisted chiefly of bringing gifts and sacrifices to the temple. The concept of sharing the goods that God entrusts to us, returning tithes and offerings to Him, is an essential part of building a faith relationship with Him. It is important because it teaches us faith—trusting Him to bless us so that the portion we keep for ourselves will be adequate for our own needs, and also teaches us to be benevolent and giving as He is with us.

If you have trouble trusting God enough to return a faithful tithe and offerings to Him now, how will you trust Him to see you through the time when only the elect will endure? Being faithful with God in the smooth times is good training for being faithful when things get rough.

Righteousness by faith is another important biblical teaching that we need to be clear on if we're to be able to maintain a strong and consistent walk with Jesus.

If you're trusting in your own works to stand you in good stead with the Lord, you'll always be getting discouraged, because you'll never feel like you're quite good enough for God to bless.

If, on the other hand, you've gone to the other side of the spectrum and decided that it doesn't really matter how you behave—you're saved by grace through faith and what you do beyond that is unimportant—then you may be missing out on a lot of the blessings God would like to send your way. If you're an "I did it my way" kind of a person who finds it hard to accept correction or instruction from God, how will it be any easier for you to follow God's leading through troublesome times? You may be setting yourself up to be one of those whose love grows cold when things get difficult.

None of us is going to make it through the times of trial in our own strength. Now is the time to settle that issue and to learn to trust in the Lord for your righteousness and to let Him work out the good works He has prepared for you to do (see Ephesians 2:10). Many Christians quote Ephesians 2:8, 9 about being saved by grace through faith, not of works, but fail to notice that verse 10 speaks of good works that God has prepared for us to do.

The Bible is well balanced in this area. It makes it clear that we can't be saved by doing good works but also points us to many good works that God wants to work through us as we grow into a closer, more trusting relationship with Him.

Forgiveness. I've already said quite a lot about this, but it's such an important aspect of the grace and truth that Jesus exemplifies that it's important to consider it again.

It's also one of the graces that many people find very difficult to practice.

But as we look to Jesus and see the way He responded even to those who struck Him and hung Him on the cross, we can see that this is a core issue in the gospel.

If we can't forgive those who wound us in small or large ways now, how will we ever be prepared to stand up on the world stage and pray for forgiveness for those who are persecuting us? And if we can't do that, how can we be a part of that final drama when all the world is waiting for that last opportunity to see the gospel fleshed out in human lives?

It is our privilege to learn from Jesus each day how to forgive those who have offended us—to live out the gospel each and every day as we prepare to portray God's grace to all the world.

Life and death. One of the things Jesus warned us would

come in the last days is a lot of false prophets, leading people astray.

One way to avoid many of the false prophetic voices that are rampant in our world today is to abide by a biblical understanding of what happens after a person dies. When Jesus spoke about Lazarus's death, He said that Lazarus was sleeping. When He raised Lazarus from the dead, He said He was going to wake him from sleep. Jesus didn't say that He was going to call Lazarus back from heaven. He was very clear that the man had gone to a state of rest.

Many deceptive prophecies today supposedly come from people who died long ago and now have come back in spirit form to communicate with a medium or a trance channeler. Proper understanding of what happens after a person dies can protect us from being led astray by these deceptive spirits.

Put plain and simply, the dead do not have the opportunity to come back and talk to us. If you receive a message from a deceased friend or relative, or a complete stranger who claims to have lived on earth and gone on to another realm, disregard it. Flee from it! You are being set up to be deceived by one of the false prophets Jesus predicted would appear in the end times.

Consistent Bible study. I could mention many other teachings and practices that God has given us in order to protect and guide us and prepare us to rightly represent Jesus in whatever trials we may face. But consistent, careful Bible study will lead you to many of these things on your own.

The life of Jesus, as recorded in the Gospels, is a good thing to focus much of your attention on. But it is also important to carefully study the prophecies. Today many appealing but inaccurate portrayals of the meaning of the prophetic portions of the Bible are being taught and preached.

Unfortunately, the majority of the Christian world is deceived on many basic points of prophetic interpretation because even mainline Protestant churches have by and large lost contact with their historic, Protestant position. This leads to misidentification of the powers we need to be watching carefully as the final events of earth's history develop. You can undertake a very helpful study of prophecy with the Discover Bible Study Guides mentioned in chapter 8.

The evidence is in

Well, the evidence is in. Jesus can still be trusted to return. We can expect Him to surprise us and to exceed our expectations.

The time is ripe for Jesus to return.

The fruit of earth's harvest is ripening.

Pray, study, and walk with Jesus daily so He can bring the fruit of His grace and truth to bear in your life as a testimony to all you come in contact with.

It is the privilege of every Christian alive today to be preparing to be a part of the group of people who will, through their consistent, grace-filled lives proclaim the gospel in the last days to all the world.

I want to be one of those who fulfill that role, don't you?

CHAPTER 10

Jesus for a New Millennium

When the time was ripe for Jesus to come to earth the first time, the people had already been through many disappointments. They had waited long, and it must have seemed to them that their hopes were never going to be fulfilled.

But the prophetic time clock was ticking away, and when the right time came, the world was prepared—even though it didn't seem like it. Despite the fact that so many rejected Jesus, the gospel spread quickly throughout the Roman Empire, because conditions were right for its dissemination. Its wide spread assured its preservation until it could be carried to the rest of the world.

The gospel has continued to spread through the years, but now we have finally arrived at a time when the fleshed-out good news about what God wants to do in human lives can be instantly relayed to the whole world. We're also at a time when the time prophecies have all run their course. As far as we can see, there's nothing more to wait for, except perhaps for the harvest of earth to be fully ripened.

The time is ripe, the harvest is waiting.

Can we trust Jesus to come at the right time?

Let's review the character evidence we've seen:

What would Mary Magdalene say? She, and a host of

others who knew Jesus when He walked on our planet, stand before us as witnesses.

I think I can hear Mary's response, can't you? "Don't give up hope! Jesus is always true to His word. Oh yeah, He'll leave you hanging sometimes. He'll test your faith a bit—leave you wondering whether He's ever going to come through on what He promised or not. But don't give up! Keep trusting. Keep looking for Him. Keep expecting great things of Him. Because you can never expect too much! Never! He always exceeds your expectations! He will come through—with more and better than you could ever ask or expect!"

Jesus never made promises He didn't plan to keep. While we may think it's been a long time and He should have returned long ere this, we need to consider time on the cosmic scale. God has always existed and always will. Those who are redeemed from this earth will someday look back on those thousands of years as a mere blink of an eye. As the song goes "When we've been there ten thousand years, bright shining as the sun, We've no less days to sing God's praise than when we'd first begun."

But more than just trustworthy, we have found Jesus to be a caring Person. He was moved with compassion for the throngs of people who surrounded Him—He reached out and touched them, bringing healing and forgiveness. He saw them as a harvest, just waiting to be gathered into His eternally joyful kingdom. He wanted to gather them in, and He wants to return soon and take as many people as possible to live with Him for all eternity. His joy is multiplied with each and every soul that finds salvation.

We've also found Jesus to be strong and courageous. He bore up under some or the most intense torture ever inflicted on a human being without losing control of His emotions. He had the courage to go to the cross because it was what needed to be done to gather in His harvest. And that's especially good news, because it means He's strong enough to carry us through whatever we may have to endure before He returns. And never fear—as we let His Spirit control our lives, He'll give us His courage as well.

But perhaps most important of all, we've found Jesus to be gracious.

There's not a one of us who doesn't need His grace. His grace to forgive us where we've fallen short. His grace to live in us to help us deal with life's daily challenges. His grace to make us over in His gracious image.

Rejoice! As we enter the third millennium since the birth of Jesus Christ, we still have a Savior we can trust.

Jesus for a new millennium is the same Jesus we've always had.

He is a Savior sufficient for all times.

APPENDIX

What did Jesus mean when He promised that " 'some who are standing here will not taste death before they seen the Son of Man coming in his kingdom' " (Matthew 16:28, NIV)?

For the past year and a half I have been writing a devotional each week based on the life and teachings of Jesus. I e-mail the devotional at the end of the week to a list of people who have requested it. As part of that series, I wrote two devotionals focused on Jesus' words in Matthew 16:27, 28. I have struggled through the years to understand what Jesus meant, and these devotionals sum up the understanding I have come to.

Incidentally, if you have e-mail and would like to receive the devotional I send out each week, just send an e-mail to freshlook@worldnet.att.net. Please be sure to put the word "subscribe" in the subject line.

Here are those two devotionals.

Expectations—5

"For the Son of Man will come in the glory of His Father with His angels, and then He will reward each according to his works. Assuredly, I say to you, there are some standing here who shall not taste death till they see the Son of Man coming in His kingdom" (Matthew 16:27, 28).

I must admit that this has been one of the most troubling verses of the Bible to me. Jesus definitely set up a high level of expectation among

His followers when He said it. If they didn't understand exactly what He meant by it at first, certainly His later description of His coming " 'on the clouds of heaven with power and great glory' " clarified it (Matthew 24:30).

Clearly He was setting up expectation of the fulfillment of Daniel 7:13, 14: " 'I was watching in the night visions, and behold, One like the Son of Man, coming with the clouds of heaven! He came to the Ancient of Days, and they brought Him near before Him. Then to Him was given dominion and glory and a kingdom, that all peoples, nations, and languages should serve Him. His dominion is an everlasting dominion, which shall not pass away, and His kingdom the one which shall not be destroyed.' "

It was only natural that anyone who heard Jesus make these statements would expect that the Second Coming, and the establishment of His worldwide kingdom, would occur sometime during the life-span of at least one of the disciples.

The closing chapter of the gospel of John reveals that this was a widely held expectation. By the time John wrote his Gospel, he may have been the last surviving disciple, and the saying was going around among the believers that Jesus had promised John that he would not die before the Second Coming. In other words, people were no doubt watching John age and reassuring one another that the Second Coming had to be *very* soon, since John probably wouldn't live much longer. In concluding his Gospel, John made a point of putting that rumor to rest (see John 20:23).

History reveals that this is another instance where Jesus did not meet the expectations of His followers. Could it be that once again His plan was to exceed what they could even imagine?

Consider another prediction He made: " 'And this gospel of the kingdom will be preached in all the world as a witness to all the nations, and then the end will come' " (Matthew 24:14).

Oh, how the disciples longed for that prophecy to be fulfilled. How each one must have prayed for it to happen in his lifetime!

But Jesus, the Creator of the world, must have understood that what He was predicting went far beyond what the disciples could conceive in their wildest imaginations. Should He have sat down with them and explained to them that there were people thousands of miles south of there in the jungles of Africa who would one day hear the gospel preached? Should He have described to them the Maya civilization across the ocean which was, even as He spoke, entering into its prime?

Jesus knew that before His return His followers would accomplish a mission far beyond what they could ever expect of themselves. They would take the gospel to *all* the world. And so once again we see that He planned to exceed, rather than meet, the expectations of those who heard Him speak.

But we're still left with the troubling issue of what Jesus really meant when He said that some would not taste death before they saw the Son of Man coming in His kingdom.

I've heard Christians explain or rationalize away this statement in various ways, but I've never been fully satisfied until recently. I believe the Gospel writer John struggled with this issue as well, and in next week's message I want to share the solution I believe he gave.

In the meantime, consider the privilege that Christians have today. Consider that all those years ago Jesus looked down to our day—a time when we really can reach every corner of the world with the gospel in some way. And let's do what we can to take the gospel to the corner we can touch today.

Expectations—6

" 'Most assuredly, I say to you, if anyone keeps My word he shall never see death' " (John 8:51).

Talk about setting up expectations! Here you have it. In the words of Jesus Himself: Immortality to be claimed, simply by keeping His word. Never to have to worry about the end of life. To live forever, never having your body laid in a dark, cold cave to rot, awaiting the day when another relative will die and your dried up bones will be carefully gathered and stored in an ossuary to make more space in the family tomb (for such were the burial customs of the Jews in Jesus' day).

It must have been especially difficult for Mary and Martha when Lazarus died shortly after Jesus spoke these words. What must it have meant to them? Jesus' words had failed on two counts. Or did it mean that Lazarus had somehow failed to abide by the words of Jesus? Did it mean that their brother was lost forever, because of his failure?

Of course, the resurrection of Lazarus solved that mystery four days later.

But then there was Stephen. What shock waves must have ricocheted through the ranks of the believers when that faithful preacher of the gospel gazed up into heaven and actually saw Jesus seated at the right hand of God but then fell victim to mob violence!

Where had he failed? What had he neglected to keep of the words of Jesus? Human expectations called for this man of God, this faithful witness, to live forever. To never taste death at all.

Jump ahead forty or fifty years. John, the disciple whom Jesus loved, pauses to look back over his long and often difficult life. He alone remains of the twelve who walked and talked with Jesus day in and day out. Everyone else has, it seems, "tasted death."

As he looks back over his life and considers what it all has meant, there must be questions yet unanswered. Will he, indeed, live to see the Lord come again? John 21:23 makes it clear that he's not absolutely certain that he will: "Then this saying went out among the brethren that this disciple would not die. Yet Jesus did not say to him that he would not die, but, 'If I will that he remain till I come, what is that to you?' "

Nonetheless it seems that John struggled with the question of what Jesus meant by His promise about not dying. His personal quest for answers no doubt influenced him to tell the story of Lazarus, which no other gospel writer mentioned. In this story we find Jesus' followers struggling with the issue of what Jesus promises about life and death, and how He delivers on His promises.

The setting is Bethany, near Jerusalem. The story occurs near the end of Jesus' earthly ministry. Coming to Jerusalem, He soon became embroiled in controversy with the religious leaders. In the encounters recorded in John 5–10, the enmity of the establishment escalates until Jesus barely escapes with His life.

Into this highly charged setting comes the story of the death of Lazarus, and it is here that John reports the conversation and events that hold the key to our understanding of what Jesus was teaching about death.

" 'Our friend Lazarus sleeps,' " Jesus said when He knew that Lazarus was dead (John 11:11).

And only then did Jesus begin the long trek up the hill toward Jerusalem, and toward His own death.

Encountering Martha on the outskirts of Bethany, Jesus assured her " 'Your brother will rise again.' " And Martha expressed her faith—that Lazarus would indeed arise at the last day. But what troubled her was the here and now.

Jesus knew what He was going to do about the here and now for Lazarus, but, nonetheless, He took the opportunity to teach Martha, and us, something we need to know: "Jesus said to her, 'I am the resurrection and the life. He who believes in Me, though he may die, he shall live. And whoever lives and believes in Me shall never die' " (verses 25, 26).

How could He say such a thing in the presence of a woman dead center in the week of mourning that followed her brother's demise?

The shock value is lost on us, because we know the end of the story.

The statements and actions of Jesus in this story make a clear differentiation between death as we know it—what He called sleep—and final death, what John in Revelation called the "second death."

There is nothing final about the first death to the one who truly believes on Jesus and keeps His word. It is no more final than lying down to get a good night's rest.

Speaking in these terms, Jesus did not set up any false expectations when He promised that some would not taste death until He came. But to humans, whose understanding of life is, for the most part, limited to what we see this side of the grave, it seemed a heady promise that proved untrue.

But Jesus was simply challenging us to get beyond our earth fixation. To move beyond wanting Him to meet our expectations, to the point where we could let Him, once again, exceed what we could ever ask or think.

If you would like to read the rest of the devotionals in this series, I've put them on my homepage on the Worldwide Web at http://tagnet.net/spiritquest/. You'll find many other resources there as well, so if you're on the web, please stop by!